The Mindless Menace of Violence

Robert F. Kennedy's Vision and the Fierce Urgency of Now

Zachary J. Martin

Hamilton Books
A member of
The Rowman & Littlefield Publishing Group
Lanham • Boulder • New York • Toronto • Plymouth, UK

Copyright © 2009 by
Hamilton Books
4501 Forbes Boulevard
Suite 200
Lanham, Maryland 20706
Hamilton Books Acquisitions Department (301) 459-3366

Estover Road
Plymouth PL6 7PY
United Kingdom

Library of Congress Control Number: 2008944204
ISBN: 978-0-7618-4449-5 (paperback : alk. paper)
eISBN: 978-0-7618-4450-1

∞™ The paper used in this publication meets the minimum
requirements of American National Standard for Information
Sciences—Permanence of Paper for Printed Library Materials,
ANSI Z39.48—1984

For those that suffer from violence and indifference all over the world.

When a man's life is destroyed or damaged by some wound or privation of soul or body, which is due to other men's actions or negligence, it is not only his sensibility that suffers but also his aspiration toward the good. Therefore there has been sacrilege towards that which is sacred in him.

—Simone Weil

Contents

Preface

We should, I believe, beware of the pitfalls described by Taine: 'Imagine a man who sets out on a voyage equipped with a pair of spectacles that magnify things to an extraordinary degree. A hair on his hand, a spot on the tablecloth, the shifting fold of a coat, all will attract his attention; at this rate, he will not go far, he will spend his day taking six steps and will never get out of his room.' We have to get out of the room.

—Robert F. Kennedy

Today it is raining outside. It is gloomy, wet, and rather depressing. As I sit here staring at the computer screen trying to develop a thought to present regarding what I hope to bring out through this work, I am overcome with an array of emotions. As a young adult trying to get by in a fast paced society, there are times that I want to curl into a ball and hide from the world. There are times that I want to be left alone and forget about everything and everyone. But soon those feelings of anxiety and fear are wiped away by the fact that these phases of panic are so small in the greater scale of the world. At the end of the day I am healthy, my family is well, I spend my day teaching students the history of a nation that I love, and each night I have a roof over my head as I sleep. What do I have to complain about, except insignificant interruptions to my daily routine?

Still there is something missing in the deep pit of my stomach and rarely can I determine a remedy that can cure its disgust. That feeling is the emotion of indifference. As I will discuss in this book, one of the greatest crimes in civilization is the offense of apathy. Indifference is a complete lack of sympathy and a total disregard of fellow human beings. But, one may ask what does this matter and what does it have to do with me? Well, the answer is simple, everyone is guilty of indifference, in one way or another, and all are to blame for the lack of progress that society has encountered while caring for one another. My fear is that in the future, people will gradually keep caring less about one another, and with that digression in human caring, our society's ethical will may be destroyed. Yet, at the same time, I am very optimistic that our civilization can move forward with ambition. For help our society need only look to the visionaries of our past.

As a native of Massachusetts I have always been intrigued by the Kennedy legacy. While growing up I paid more attention to John F. Kennedy and his life rather than any other Kennedy. But as I grew older and more aware of the world in which I live in, I grew more attached to the legacy of Robert F. Kennedy. He was an incredible human being. Like everyone, he had human frailties and individual flaws, but he used his worldly ambition to try to move the world to change so that the suffering that eclipsed happiness might be erased. His ability to try and see the best in humanity was a wonderful characteristic. One can only hope that they can use their life to help those that cannot help themselves, and move forward even in the face of difficulty and improbability. If our society does this the hope for the future will be secure.

While enrolled at the University of Connecticut in the spring of 2008, I took a seminar on the American Revolution, hoping to gain a greater understanding of the founding of our nation. While reading one of the books assigned for the course, I came across a story that I feel appropriate to add now. I read that after the American Revolution had ended, Benjamin Franklin set out to complete his autobiography. Franklin tackled the project with the intent of instructing his fellow Americans to achieve moral perfection. He took his project very seriously, but he was not asking for the people to work towards "utopian virtues," which required a complete change of one's worldly intent. Rather he asked for Americans to achieve realistic objectives that not only saints could achieve, but ordinary people as well. Some of the virtues that he asked people to work towards were sincerity, justice, tranquility, humility, and more. In order to successfully discuss this process of achieving moral perfection, he used an anecdote known as the "speckled ax." Gordon S. Wood discussed this same anecdote in his work, *The Americanization of Benjamin Franklin*, and eloquently added Franklin's thoughts. He stated,

A man bought a new ax and now wanted to have the whole surface of his ax as bright as the edge. The smith who had sold him the ax consented to grind it bright for him if the man would turn the wheel. The smith pressed the broad face of the ax hard and heavy against the stone, which made turning it very fatiguing. The man, becoming more and more tired, kept leaving the wheel to see how the grinding was coming. Finally, the exhausted man declared he would take his ax as it was without further grinding. No, said the smith, keep turning and sooner or later we'll have it bright; as yet, it was still only speckled. 'Yes, says the man; but – *I think I like a speckled ax best.*'[1]

As Franklin asked his readers to understand, this was the way people rationalized abandoning their efforts. He wanted people to break their bad habits and establish good ones. People all too often follow the gentleman's lead and give up the struggle concluding, "that *a speckled ax was best.*" The individual did not really like that ax best, he just did not want to work hard to achieve the result he had originally envisioned. During his lifetime Benjamin Franklin did not attain the moral perfection that he sought. Still, his work to create a better world was worth the journey. Therefore, let our society follow his lead and not follow the individual that gave up.

I am not asking everyone to live their entire lives in pursuit of moral perfection. I understand that the idea of utopia is difficult, if even possible, to attain. Even so, that should not mean that society should live to that realization. All of us can move forward and live our lives just a little bit better. Violence in society today is truly beginning to become an appalling story. When one turns on the television and hears of more violent deaths, gang assaults, and beatings, they become ashamed and appalled at our society. Recently stories from places like Providence, Rhode Island have shown a new phenomenon in our society, beatings captured on video camera and broadcast to the world. Society can now watch as teenagers beat helpless and innocent young adults on camera and post it on internet devices like "*Youtube.*" This is a serious degeneration of ethics and morals in American society. How can anyone get enjoyment out of the torturing and beating of others? There seems to be a serious lack of empathy in today's society. This is such a horrible problem, but it continues unchallenged.

Recently I went on the internet and observed a news story which discussed how a man was hit by a car in Hartford, Connecticut. The person that hit the individual drove away and bystanders did nothing except watch. When they grew bored of just watching as an injured man lie motionless on the ground they proceeded to walk away. They acted indifferent to his pain and suffering and instead focused on their own personal time. Finally after a few minutes some people began to check to see if the man was alright, but not before several cars had driven around the man and went about their business uncaring of who they were trying to get around.

In the midst of unconceivable violence, our society has seen in the last eight years a governing power that has abused its power and made this country a difficult place to live in. This nation's beacon of hope has faded in the last eight years through needless war, terrible economic polices, denial of global warming, opposition to stricter gun control laws, denial of universal health care, and has strengthened the drop out rate in high schools throughout the nation with the no-child left behind policy. Today's nation not only has to worry about the crimes of those around us, but the crimes committed by those that are supposed to lead this nation with moral leadership. For the last eight years there has been no moral leadership and instead a presidency based on mismanagement. Yet, in 2008, the beacon of light that has faded into darkness has begun to see light again as our country enters into a new election season, with the knowledge that the Constitution will not allow the current president to run again. His departure must be our society's chance to build a better nation with ethical leadership.

Through it all, it is our society that must carry the torch of what Kennedy envisioned was to be done to combat violence in American society and throughout the world. Our nation must not act as a bully in the world, creating more enemies and alienating friends, but rather lead with the understanding that our goal is the hope of all. Americans want to live in a world free of oppression and without fear. They no longer want to be the ones that perpetrate the very violence they seek to end. Our nation has a past filled with wisdom, ambition, and success. It is time that our society look back and reflect on those great Americans that have dedicated their lives to creating a nation dedicated to human justice. When people look back for hope and when our society looks to the past for help, they look to people like Robert F. Kennedy.

When Robert Kennedy spoke in Cleveland in 1968, the day after Martin Luther King Jr. was assassinated, he spoke of what troubled him and what troubled the nation he loved. The message he presented then is important to our society today and will be important for future generations. The gift of his character and the legacy of his ambition are qualities that our nation must recognize and desire to become. He spoke from the heart and told a troubled nation what they needed to hear. Our nation has problems with many sectors and together must combat these issues. Violence is one of the biggest problems affecting our society and through its treachery many other problems follow in line. Robert Kennedy's words in 1968 can be looked at today as a guiding light. This work serves as a bridge. It brings a crucial speech that Robert Kennedy gave in 1968 to those that live now and have still yet to be born. It is a book dedicated to those that suffer. It is a book that aims to inform and educate everyone about what is wrong with society and how it can still be changed. Lastly, this is a book devoted to the vision that Robert Kennedy had and a reminder that the dream he helped build will never die.

The Mindless Menace of Violence: Robert F. Kennedy's Vision and the Fierce Urgency of Now is about the speech that Robert Kennedy gave and the message it brings to every generation of human beings. Our society can learn a lot from the vision of Robert Kennedy and the words he provided regarding the problem of violence and indifference in society. The problems he spoke of did only not affect the 1960s. These same issues affect our society today. Therefore, what he said can be read today as if it were written today. The power of his words must be understood, but the saddest part is the knowledge that things have not changed. The point of the speech and this work is to show that it is never too late to change and bring happiness to those in pain. Each of us can work to change the world. With one small step Americans can build a road to a better world for future generations. With love for one another, caring for one another, ending fear of one another, and working with one another the possibilities of our ambitions become endless.

This is the task that *The Mindless Menace of Violence: Robert F. Kennedy's Vision and the Fierce Urgency of Now* asks of its reader. Respect the words of Robert Kennedy, recognize the problems that affect our society, and work together to change the course of human events with courage and affection. I cannot speak for society, but I am tired of turning on the television or reading the news and seeing countless stories of needless deaths from violent acts of indifference or needless war. The terrible stories remind us that many problems affect our nation and everyone must work together with the wisdom of our past to create a world free of fear and want. Therefore let us start with the reading and appreciation of a speech that with its words can change the possibilities of hope.

Zachary J. Martin
Boston, Massachusetts
June 29, 2008

NOTES

1. Gordon S. Wood, *The Americanization of Benjamin Franklin*, (New York: The Penguin Press HC, 2004), 205-206.

Foreword

I like the dreams of the future, rather than the history of the past. So good-night, I will dream on.

—Thomas Jefferson

As a young historian, one learns very quickly that there are certain components to every society that plague it and contribute to its downfall. Rome fell victim to leaders who grew too power hungry and corrupt. The Ottoman Empire was the victim of internal conflict and the inability to conform to new ideas. Two great empires that seemingly ruled with authority and lived prosperously, in the end fell in a relatively short time.

These great empires, and many others like them, were once regarded as the standard for the rest of the world to attain in terms of a successful human civilization. Many would argue today that America perhaps is the standard for living. Whether this is a self perception or the view of the world, America today is at a crossroads. The prosperity of life after the Second World War has eluded the members of today's society. The safe streets, the standard of education, and the family unit have changed so drastically and so quickly that America has been left in a state of confusion. Leadership is visible but baffling. Taxes are high but squandered. Violence is becoming more prominent and crimes more heinous.

If this is the state of affairs, what then should be done to avoid the fate of other societies? Historians and sociologists in their classrooms, or in their own academic works, metaphorically scream and yell to those they educate that society must take a long hard look at its past to find the instances they must not repeat in order to avoid the vicious cycle of history. Politicians and citizens must not neglect the statistics. Historians shout "if nothing changes, history is bound to repeat itself." Yet, the same mistakes and errors in judgment occur. Maya Angelou once remarked, "History, despite its wrenching pain, cannot be unlived, but if faced with courage, need not be lived again."

In *The Mindless Menace of Violence: Robert F. Kennedy's Vision and the Fierce Urgency of Now*, Zachary J. Martin attempts an option that does one better than his peers. In this historical sociological hybrid, this work aims not to simply point out the problems in society today but offer guidance through the words of one of the most influential and amazing American political figures in the countries short history in the form of Robert F. Kennedy. Through one public speech, Kennedy outlined a guide explaining the factors that were contributing to the growth of violence as well as offered unifying words that pushed society to search for action and answers. Martin brilliantly interprets this plan for change while offering his own insights and examples amongst the words of other great men like Martin Luther King Jr., Abraham Lincoln, and Patrick Henry.

Martin does not, much like his hero Kennedy, offer all the answers to the epidemic of violence, rather uses his muse, history, to demand that America take a good long look in the mirror and then open the dialogue for change. He challenges Americans to hold up their end of the societal bargain. He aptly cites and explains the urges of great historical figures of past generations as encouragement for the brave journey this country must attempt.

The Mindless Menace of Violence: Robert F. Kennedy's Vision and the Fierce Urgency of Now is a stellar contribution to both fields and will speak to the young American as well as wake up older citizens to what has become of this country in terms of violence. It is an important contribution, as Martin reminds us that history will judge this time in America. Everyone must believe that it is possible to avoid becoming a rise and fall society among the pages of history.

> Corinne M. Richard
> Professor at Salem State College
> Salem, Massachusetts

Acknowledgments

Men of authority and influence may promote good morals. Let them in
their several stations encourage virtue . . . let them favor and take part in
any plans which may be formed for the advancement of morality.

—William Wilberforce

This work would not have been completed without the help of many helpful
and cooperative people that found something very special and wonderful in
this book. First I would just like to thank *The Roman & Littlefield Publishing
Group* and their affiliates, *The University Press of America, Inc.* and *Hamilton Books* for publishing this work and believing in its merit and vision.
Thank you to Samantha Kirk for her help at *The University Press of America*
and *Hamilton Books* in getting this work published. Her insight and ideas
were a valuable addition, as was her belief in this work. Tremendous thanks
to the editing staff and marketing staff at *Hamilton Books.* Thanks to Brian
DeRocco, Amanda Slaybaugh, the graphic design team and Judith L. Rothman, Vice President and director of *Hamilton Books* and the *University Press
of America*, as well for their work in publishing this work and marketing it to
all those interested in its possibility.

Of course special thanks must again be given to Corinne M. Richard for all
her help editing and critiquing this work. This is the second time we have
worked together in publication. Her work was a fantastic contribution and exceeds her editing skills and her love of politics and social change. The work
she did behind the scenes such as getting the book published and marketed,
as well as moral support, was of extreme importance and truthfully I could
not have finished this book without her. The message of Robert Kennedy
gave us both the opportunity to tackle some of the most important issues of

today and provide our feelings and insight. Having Ms Richard during this journey was invaluable and this work is as just as much hers as it is mine.

A special thank you must also go to Mr. Bill Eppridge. Mr. Eppridge is a graduate of the University of Missouri where he received a bachelor's degree in journalism. He is a former photojournalist for *National Geographic* and *Life* magazine. He is revered as one of the best photojournalists in our nation's history. Mr. Eppridge had the kindness and decency to allow me to use one of his famous photos of Robert Kennedy taken in 1966 on the cover of *The Mindless Menace of Violence: Robert F. Kennedy's Vision and the Fierce Urgency of Now*. It is an honor to have his photo on the cover of this work. It could not have been a more perfect photo of the late senator and presidential hopeful. Mr. Eppridge is a man of character and has taken photos that have had a profound effect on Americans of past generations, this generation, and will assuredly affect those of future generations. I owe him thanks and appreciation for the use of his photo and hope this work honors the legacy of someone that meant a great deal to him.

Thanks must also go out to those individuals and organizations that have helped me in my continued research. I would like to extend my gratitude to Karren Allen, who sponsored me and supported me in presenting my work in a keynote lecture at the New Bedford Whaling Museum on January 10, 2008. Karren has been a tremendous supporter of my work. She has asked me to speak at the Whaling Museum on several occasions and has allowed to me spread the wealth of history to many communities. Thank you to the New Bedford Whaling Museum, New Bedford Public Library, New Bedford Historical Society, Fairhaven Millicent Library, Bristol Community College, University of Massachusetts Dartmouth, Providence College, the University of Connecticut, and the John F. Kennedy Library for use of their research facilities and archives. A special thanks to their experienced staff of associates, who were a tremendous help while doing research for this book.

To the many people that have helped and supported me along the way and inspired me to write a book that wakes up our sleeping society in regards to the many issues that plague our people. Thank you to Len Travers for his support, guidance, and mentorship in my pursuit of history. Thank you to Erich Carroll for his wisdom and guidance. Thank you to Heather Albritton and Ralph Tripp for their compassion and continued support of me in chasing my dreams. Great thanks to Dr. Richard Potter from Roger Williams University for his support and leadership. Great thanks to the students that I have had the pleasure of teaching at Roger Williams University and Bristol Community College. Thank you to Dr. Fred Rocco and Maggie O'Brian for their continued support at Bristol Community College. Special thanks to the history departments at the University of Massachusetts Dartmouth and Providence College. Special thanks to Dr. Paul O'Malley, Dr. Mark Vaughn, Dr. Matthew Dowling, Dr. Richard Grace, and Dr. William Leeman.

Last, but by far not least, a special thanks to those loved ones that have supported me in following the vision and passion that I have continued to live by. Thanks to my mother Deborah Devlin, my brother Bobby, my sister Rebecca and my father Robert Martin. Thanks to my brother Jeff and his wife Lauren. Special thanks to Corinne M. Richard and her mother Mary, her father Patrick, her brother Kyle and her sister Kaitlyn. Thanks to Linda and Sonny Tice, and Brian and Maegan Tice. To my family and friends: Ronald and Sybil Almieda, Ronnie Almieda, Kristen and David Slater, Frank and Madeline Edwards, Michael Edwards, Christopher and Anne Mauriello, Frederick Mauriello and Mary Louse, Margie Mauriello, Lisa and Larry Charland, Gus Richard and the Richard family, Donald Knapman, Joe Motta, Makna Men, Jennifer Clifford, Jane Newburt-Avila, Lucy Resendes, Rosamaria Carlozzi, Lisa Jimenez, Crystal Dutra, Carey Greenway and her family, Ivo Luis, Kosta Erotokretakis, Lisa Thatcher, Ray Oliver, Christopher and Christine Kobza, Sandy Eckenreiter and her family, and Peter Magalhaes and his family. For those family members and friends that are not mentioned, I send you thanks with love. Without all of those mentioned, the vision and hope of this book would have been much harder to form. For this I am thankful. Ending with a thanks to all those that have provided a helping hand and could not be here to see the rewards of their efforts. To them I am indebted and forever grateful. I only hope this book lives up to their expectations.

Chapter One

The Stain of Bloodshed Has Spread

Violence is not merely killing another. It is violence when we use a sharp word, when we make a gesture to brush away a person, when we obey because there is fear. So violence isn't merely organized butchery in the name of God, in the name of society or country. Violence is much more subtle, much deeper, and we are inquiring into the very depths of violence.

—Jiddu Krishnamurti

On the morning of Tuesday April 20, 1999, at Columbine High School in Jefferson County, Colorado near Littleton, two students named Dylan Klebold and Eric Harris went on a shooting rampage, which resulted in the deaths of twelve students and one teacher including twenty-four injuries. The carnage only ended when both young men took their own lives. At that point it was ranked as the second worst school shooting in American history behind the school shooting at the University of Texas in 1966. During ninety-six minute's of terror, Charles Whitman fired his "6mm rifle" at students from the University of Texas clock tower. In the aftermath of this carnage, fourteen people were killed and thirty-one wounded. Whitman was killed when police raided the tower. However, the Columbine and University of Texas shootings would be outdone on April 16, 2007 on the college campus of Virginia Tech, where Seung-Hui Cho carried out the worst school shooing in American history by killing thirty-two of his fellow students and professors. He then turned the gun on himself.

Violence does not only occur in the innocent classrooms of America's elementary, middle, high school, or even college campuses. Violence can be felt and seen by all, no matter where they live. In the history of the United States, violence has strangled the country and brought a proud standing nation to its knees in sorrow. Countless acts of violence have been inflicted on the American

1

landscape and have been felt in every corner of the nation. From Oklahoma City, to September 11th, from the civil rights riots of the 1960s, to the Kent State Massacre in 1970, from gang violence to organized crime, to the assassinations of political leaders to brutal killings of innocent civilians, Americans have seen violence in their country rise to appalling heights. Even so, America is not alone with its history of violence or separate from other nations with the belief and understanding that measures must be taken to make this world a safer place for all human beings. History is riddled with acts of violence. When one person is killed, the flame of ambition that burns within their heart is doused with blood. With the loss of this hope, the nation is saddened. The world has the ability to be cured from this ailment. Who has the moral courage to stand up against this enemy?

There are many people in this world that believe that there is nothing that can be done to sway the growing tide of violence. There are those that look to comfortable answers and demand that human beings have always used violence and therefore will always be violent. In all reality this is a pessimistic approach to solving the world's problems and allows the purveyors of evil to win. In that same vein, many cite history as a symbol for the future and with it an outlook and acceptance for a depressing end to their generation and future generations. Yet, while history can be used to express doubt for the future, it can also be used to convey hope and appreciation. There have been many people that have refused to accept that human nature will remain as it is or as it has been. Influential political leaders throughout history have expressed optimism in the future and faith in the conscience of human beings.

When it comes to American history there is a wonderful optimism for the future, but at the same time an understanding that the time has come for society to change. Today America has come to that moment, where it can either move forward working to create a better place to live, or remain unchanged through inaction. While the latter may be easier and the outcome known, the former holds promise. It gives a nation and its people the ability to shape their legacy and how future societies judge them. Is this going to be an era that allows for future historians and analysts to look back with disgust saying, "Why did they not do more for the environment? Why did they not stop the violence devastating their society? How could they have been so selfish?" Or, will they look at our society with admiration and thanks? Our society must not move forward looking back at our legacy, but simply onward to our future. Therefore, our history has yet to be written and while Americans look to our past for help with answers for today's issues, it still must be understood that wrong choices have been made and those are what must be avoided now.

The history of America was created on the freedoms of speech, religion, and press. It is a nation founded on the idea of individual liberty and democratic principles, and in that same idea it is a history stimulated by growth. The United States fought to gain independence and create a nation free from unjust colonial rule. Americans worked together to create the Constitution and form a United States based on concepts of autonomy and equality. Yet, the United States failed to live up to its promise to a portion of Americans not able to enjoy many basic rights. While the history of the United States has been encompassed with many glowing and heart wrenching instances, the issue of violence in American society is best discussed by beginning in the 1950s. Although, Robert Kennedy's "Mindless Menace of Violence" speech was given in 1968, the speech was in part directed at the civil rights movement and the growing racial violence in the country between black and white Americans. Therefore, by starting with the 1950s the major issues that Kennedy attacked and the leaders that he called friend and brother can be examined and discussed.

The 1950s witnessed the rapid growth of the civil rights movement and an end to segregation in schools, with *Brown vs. the Board of Education of Topeka, Kansas*, and ending social public segregation. Rosa Parks defied the law and rode in the front of the bus and through her courage shook the core of southern oppression to its knees. This decade also saw fear of communism grow to incredible numbers as many Americans were afraid that communism would topple democracy. It was a decade of growing developments in weaponry and humans discovered more ways to kill each other, or at least threaten to kill each other.

In the opposite idea, the 1950s were a time of great success. The economic structure of America had finally begun to regain its position since the end of the 1920s and because of America's positions during and after the Second World War, it was an extremely prosperous time. The microwave was developed, television was becoming a societal norm and most people began to get their information from television rather than from the radio. Women began to gain more societal equality, already gaining the right to vote in the 1920s. Women were then ready to break free from the chain of the home and prepared to become a part of the changing society. Nonetheless, their ability to change their social status was stunted and their search for individuality not yet possible.

While the 1950s saw the baby boom, the suburban boom, and the economic boom, the future appeared to be extremely bright, even in the face of severe international problems with the Soviet Union and the threat of communism along side the continued possibility of nuclear war. With the 1950s coming to a close and the 1960s quickly approaching, young Americans were ready to take power and bring the country to a "New Frontier" in human civilization.[1] If the 1950s were characterized as prosperous and conventional, the 1960s were conversely a time of chaos and disenfranchisement. An era that began with optimism, aspiration, and the leadership of a new generation, society would soon have this same hope grow sour.

In 1960, the youngest person ever elected president was chosen by only 100,000 popular votes and became the 35th President of the United States of America. John Fitzgerald Kennedy, Democratic Senator from Massachusetts, out paced his opponent, Republican Vice-President Richard Millhouse Nixon. In an age when television was becoming a popular entertainment device, it was also becoming an important political tool. In 1960, the first televised debate was held showing a very well presented, handsome, and charismatic Kennedy as opposed to an aging, sweating, and confused Nixon.[2] John F. Kennedy represented the young hope of the country. He was a man that had served with distinction as a P.T. boat commander in the South Pacific during World War II and a man brought up with wealth and luxury. For the first time in American history a man born in the twentieth-century and had entered political office after the Second World War had been elected president. He was young, married to a beautiful woman named Jacqueline Bouvier, and brought with him an essence of American royalty and was displayed as a symbol for a decade he ushered in and what his wife would later call an era of "Camelot."[3]

Camelot itself is neither a myth nor a factual reality. It is in truth the idea of something precious, something almost too incredible to speak of, and lastly something unbelievable. Camelot is something one can sense but once he or she tries to obtain it, it is gone. It is too fragile for human touch. Kennedy's presidency lasted only one thousand days, but within that brief span of time he presented many ambitious policies for the American people. He pushed for the development of Medicare, Medicaid, progression with the Department of Urban Housing, development of the Peacecorps, services for the mentally handicapped, and lastly pushed for stronger civil rights for African Americans. However, most of these he failed to enact. When it came to the advancement of civil rights, Kennedy was slow to act in the beginning of his presidency, but major events during his term in office moved him to act and call for the problems of civil rights to be looked at as a "moral issue."

When James Meredith applied for admission to the University of Mississippi in 1962, he was met with strong opposition from the southern political sphere. Kennedy, Attorney General Robert F. Kennedy, and Ross Barnett, Governor of Mississippi, worked closely to avoid a violent encounter. Although Barnett had promised cooperation with the Kennedy's, violence erupted the night before Meredith was set to enroll. The United States Marshals and the National Guard were attacked by a vicious mob. The result of the mob violence left two individuals dead and three hundred and seventy injured. Although the violence could not be avoided, emotions calmed down and Meredith enrolled in class eventually graduating from the University of Mississippi.

With the event that transpired in Mississippi, Kennedy knew that the time was drawing closer to when he would have to make a serious stand on the civil rights issue and finally push Congress to act, but still he refused to present a bill to Congress. That would all change with an incident that took place in Birmingham, Alabama. Martin Luther King, Jr., the symbolic leader of the civil rights movement, was the main person that forced Kennedy to finally act. In 1963, King brought his fight to the most segregated city in the South, Birmingham.[4] There he staged massive protests and marches, all of which aimed at taking down segregation and discrimination. Many supporters were arrested, including King. The man in charge of trying to crush the civil right's demonstrators was police commissioner Eugene "Bull" Connor. King and Connor would have a final clash.

On May 3, 1963, six thousand children marched on the streets of Birmingham because most of the adult protestors had already been jailed.[5] The nonviolent protestors were met on the streets by police who used clubs, snarling dogs, and fire hoses to break up their demonstrations. All of the brutality that took place that day was being televised for the world to see, and quickly civil rights became a national and international issue.[6] Kennedy, who also witnessed the violence on television, quickly acted to stop the brutality, and demanded that the political leaders in Birmingham grant the demands of the demonstrators. The following month, June of 1963, Alabama became the next location of concern for Kennedy and civil rights. Governor George Wallace refused to allow two black students to enter the University of Alabama. Kennedy used the National Guard to ensure the safety of the students and to make sure that they were able to attend classes.[7] It was at this time that Kennedy ended his "tip toeing" around the civil rights issue.

On June 11, 1963, he called on Congress to act, speaking to the nation on television to discuss his hopes for racial equality. He stated,

Good evening my fellow citizens . . . This nation was founded by men of many nations and backgrounds. It was founded on the principle that all men are created equal, and that the rights of every man are diminished when the rights of one man are threatened.[8]

When Thomas Jefferson was instructed to pen the Declaration of Independence, he wrote that "all men are created equal." Whether Jefferson believed that free blacks and slaves were a part of the bigger picture of equality has been debated for generations, but as written and as future generations fought for, his words meant equal opportunity for all. When one man's rights are taken away in order to advance the rights of another, society loses a sense of the very idea of freedom. Freedom must not be taken for granted, and humans must not willingly hand over the same freedoms that throughout the years many have died to secure. Governments and their leaders must not be allowed to use their power and influence to take away the rights of the people, even to heighten the safety of all.

As John F. Kennedy said, when society diminishes our rights for whatever reason given, this threatens the rights of all. If someone willingly makes that move, no one knows when, or if, that move will end. John F. Kennedy continued,

> Today we are committed to a worldwide struggle to promote and protect the rights of all who wish to be free. And when Americans are sent to Vietnam or West Berlin, we do not ask for whites only. It ought to be possible; therefore, for American students of any color to attend any public institution they select without having to be backed up by troops . . . It ought to be possible, in short, for every American to enjoy the privileges of being American without regard to his race or his color. In short, every American ought to have the right to be treated as he would wish to be treated, as one would wish his children to be treated. But this is not the case.[9]

The point that Kennedy was trying to get across in this speech was that America no longer should function as a nation suffering from racial discrimination. Ironically, America at this time was pledging support to citizens of other nations like Vietnam and West Berlin, Germany, and the soldiers being sent there to protect those people were not only white but black. If Americans that are black can protect other nation's citizens then they too should be protected in the place they call home. African Americans needed to be treated with dignity and respect. It was important that they be allowed to attend any college or school of their choosing and gain the educational training so easily open to those citizens with a lighter skin tone. In the last analysis, African Americans and other minorities, as well as those suffering from economic duress, needed to be secure in their hope to live a life better than their parents. In that same vein, these individuals should be able to provide a life better than their own for their children. The color of one's skin should not be what drives a man to fail or lose hope, but rather race must play no role in how society functions.

As Kennedy conveyed, in American society, race plays a major role, but that was the major problem, because race should be a non-issue. Kennedy continued,

> The Negro baby born in America today, regardless of the section of the nation in which he is born, has about one-half as much chance of completing high school as a white baby born in the same place on the same day, one-third as much chance of completing college, one-third as much chance of becoming a professional man, twice as much chance of becoming unemployed . . . a life expectancy which is seven years shorter, and the prospects of earning only half as much. This is not a sectional issue. Difficulties over segregation and discrimination exist in every city, in every state of the union; producing in many cities a

rising tide of discontent that threatens the public safety…We are confronted primarily with a moral issue. It is as old as the scriptures and is as clear as the American Constitution.[10]

A society that sees a portion of its men, women, and children unable to take advantage of a great country because of race, is a clear indication of failure at the highest level. The statistics that Kennedy gave in this piece were heart wrenching and unacceptable in any society. He even asserts that these issues of racial discrimination affect every city and state in the United States, and he was not wrong. He sees that this injustice in American society will only grow to serious discontent in civilization if it was not fixed. Kennedy knew that this was no longer a singular political issue, but a moral issue that was as clear as day and must be remedied.

As Kennedy addressed the American people regarding the problem of racial discrimination in American society he attempted to paint parallels with the Civil War generation. He continued,

Who among us would then be content with the counsels of patience and delay? One hundred years of delay have passed since President Lincoln freed the slaves, yet their heirs, their grandsons, are not fully free. They are not yet freed from the bonds of injustice. They are not yet freed from social and economic oppression. And this nation, for all its hopes and all its boasts, will not be fully free until all its citizens are free.[11]

Kennedy called to mind the name Lincoln and in so doing invoked the legacy of his moral leadership. By citing Abraham Lincoln, Kennedy gave the audience an example of a person entrusted with the same power over the nation as he had been trusted with. Lincoln had been commander and chief during this nation's most difficult time, the Civil War. At this point, Kennedy used his name to show how chaotic the problems of the country had been and were allowed to fester. He discussed that the descendents of the slaves that were freed under Lincoln were still not free. Yes, free in that there was no institution of slavery, but still lacking freedom in the sense of how all Americans, both white and black, interpret this idea. Injustice was rampant and social and economic opportunities were taken away negatively from minorities in society in the 1960s. As Kennedy stated, America may brag about its beauty, its freedom, and its abilities, but America will not be fully free until all its citizens can boast that they are free. As Kennedy closed his remarks,

Now the time has come for this nation to fulfill its promise . . . The fires of frustration and discord are burning in every city, North and South, where legal remedies are not at hand. Redress is sought in the streets, in demonstrations, parades and protests which create tensions and threaten violence and threaten lives. We face, therefore, a moral crisis as a country and as a people.[12]

Legal measures were needed to curtail the violence that Kennedy saw on the horizon, and yet still today this level of violence continues. Kennedy felt that if this division was allowed to grow, then the threat of fear and violence would be the child of indifference. As he concluded his speech, the country had come to the crossroads. As Lincoln realized, could this nation coexist as a nation where some were free and others were not? It was an ethical crisis and everyone in the country was a part of it.

As Kennedy demanded Congress act, the civil rights movement itself refused to wait for the government to provide them with an answer to their problem, which Kennedy warned would happen. On August 28, 1963, more than 200,000 demonstrators gathered in Washington D.C. for a rally on the front steps of the Lincoln Memorial. There the demonstrators listened to speeches, music, and prayed for an end to racial discrimination and human injustice. What better place to hold a rally than at the footsteps of the memorial dedicated to a man that had helped free the slaves one hundred years earlier. There at his feet, supporters called on the country to live up to the obligations, which Lincoln himself had asked the country to grant, rights for African Americans. For one-hundred years since Lincoln enacted the Emancipation Proclamation, African Americans had been denied their civil and human rights. King demanded a change in policy.

The one thing about American history that is perpetual is the written word. When one reads about history and does research, primary documents can be the most valuable source of information. In that same respect nothing gives historians a greater sense of the time studied than speeches. Speeches passed down from generation to generation about a major event, law, or campaign of that era allow one to read about those individuals and their intentions or the plan for the future of the country. President Kennedy had many great speeches and might have had many more, but on November 22, 1963 he was assassinated by a bullet at the hands of Lee Harvey Oswald in Dallas, Texas. With his death the major idea behind this work begins to take shape, it is an understanding of violence in American society. The death of President Kennedy ended the hope of the 1960s, ended the idea of an American "Camelot," but began an era of unprecedented violence in American society that would not end until after 1968. Looking around today, many wonder if the level of violence that inflicted so much pain in the 1960s has ever actually stopped.

The loss of John F. Kennedy was a huge devastation to the United States. After Lyndon B. Johnson took over as the 36th President of the United States he was able to pass, in memory of the late president, the Civil Rights Act of 1964 and the Voting Rights Act of 1965, stopping discrimination in public accommodations and securing black Americans the right to vote, respectively.[13]

He took it upon himself to take on poverty in America and secure the advancement of the country through domestic polices. Soon after, unfortunately, the war in Vietnam began to demand more attention and money, causing domestic polices to take a back seat to the conflict in Indochina.

By 1968, the violence in the United States had reached an unprecedented level and cost the lives of a few of the countries greatest activists. On April 3, 1968, Martin Luther King was in the city of Memphis, Tennessee to fight for the rights of black sanitation workers who were being paid substantially lower wages as compared to white workers.[14] He gave a speech that evening to faithful listeners. The title of his speech would come to be known famously as the "Mountaintop Speech."[15] He discussed that evening of his wish to have the nation he loved direct its course on how citizens treated one another. In the course of his speech, Martin Luther King Jr. used the story of the "Good Samaritan" to paint a picture of how he felt society had been going about its daily routine. He spoke of the issue of indifference, which will be explained in depth in later chapters.

The idea of indifference is that people are becoming more inclined not to care about their fellow human beings. King felt that people for the most part were afraid of their neighbors and not willing to provide a helping hand when needed. He discussed how a priest and Levite paid no attention to an injured man lying helpless in the middle of the road because they were worried about their safety from those that had hurt the man on the ground.[16] Therefore they used their own fear to look the other way and refused to help the injured man. As King also describes, both individuals also wondered if the man on the ground was faking in order to rob or hurt them. As a man that King calls the "Good Samaritan" comes along, he cares not what will happen to him if he stops to help, but rather what will happen to the man on the ground if he just walks away.[17] King asked everyone to begin to care about everyone like they cared about themselves. He asked everyone to stop fearing the unknown and instead brave the depths of human compassion. As French journalist, philosopher and Nobel Prize winner Albert Camus stated,

> We are faced with evil. I feel rather like Augustine did before becoming a Christian when he said, "I tried to find the source of evil and I got nowhere. But it is also true that I and a few others knew what must be done if not to reduce evil at least not to add to it." Perhaps we cannot prevent this world from being a world in which children are tortured. But we can reduce the number of tortured children. And if you believers don't help us, who else in the world can help us do this?[18]

Everyone must act and work to help everyone and reduce the number of crimes and evils that occur in society. Everyone must act as the "Good Samaritan" acted and as Camus understood people should act, with compassion, courage, and generosity.

A personal relation of this concept can be illustrated through an experience that a friend of mine had not long ago. In April of 2008 that friend was stopped at a red light and saw a man standing on the side of the street begging for some money because he could not afford to feed himself. As that individual sat there, she pondered the same moral question, which King had mused over. Everyone else rolled up their windows, locked their doors, turned up their music, or blatantly ignored the individual as he stood on the corner, hoping someone could give him only a dollar. The wonderful part of this story is that like Martin Luther King and many others, this individual cared more about the person going hungry than her own personal security, her money, or her time. She got out of the car, went over to the man and provided him with all she had in her purse. After being given the money, the gentlemen looked at her teary eyed and thanked her for her kindness, saying that she was the only person all day that had given him anything other than a dirty look. She stopped to help that individual and society today must follow her lead as well as the message of King.

King used the message of the "Good Samaritan" to explain why he was in Memphis trying to protect the rights of sanitation workers. While thinking of the inured man in the middle of the road, King also pondered the irony around him. He came to the same conclusion regarding the small class of workers in Memphis, Tennessee as the "Good Samaritan" had pondered regarding the helpless man on the side of the road. Instead of walking by a down trodden neighbor unaware or uncaring of their problem, provide them with assistance rather than fearing what could happen by stopping. Society must consider instead what might happen to their neighbor if he or she does nothing at a time when they are needed the most. King asked everyone to stop caring about the time that might be lost when someone aids another or the work that goes unfinished when an individual lends a helping hand to a fellow citizen, rather King asked for nothing less than action.[19]

Action was King's remedy to the serious lack of concern in society and the need to withdraw from the world because of fear. He used this as a parallel to explain to the people of America why he was helping sanitation workers. King believed they deserved better pay and better working conditions just like the president of a major business, and people must respect their need for those rights. This was why King was there. If Americans allowed their rights to be infringed upon and conditions to worsen, where would the sorrow end? Not knowing was enough for King to act to protect the sanitation workers and provide his time to their cause. In reality their causes were intertwined and connected to one another. The fight to protect their rights as free men can best be expressed as the fight that everyone must continue today for the homeless, those without medical insurance, those victims of violence and those ready to live in a country that lives up to the highest moral standard. As Albert Camus once stated so eloquently,

> The oppressed want to be liberated not only from their hunger but also from their masters. They are well aware that they will be effectively freed of hunger when they hold their masters, all their masters, at bay.[20]

Thomas Jefferson once stated that when a people, a country, or a society is placed under new circumstances, it will call for "new words, new phrases and for the transfer of old words to new objects." King understood Jefferson's message and called on everyone to change the way they looked at the problems affecting society. As the brilliant preacher that King was, his sermon that evening provided generations with the call to help their neighbor and live their lives dedicated to moral and sound principles. Towards the end of his speech King also discussed the time he was in New York signing autographs and was stabbed by a "demented black women."[21] Through his interpretation of such a profound moment in his life, King was able to bring the audience back to that fateful day and show that his life was never secured or guaranteed. At one point everything had almost been taken away from him, and if he had died he would have missed many incredible moments for the civil rights movement. He discussed that he could easily have died and with his death the movement towards equality could have changed.

As King discussed, the most important thing about the assassination was that he had survived and come within an inch of dying. While in the hospital he received hundreds of letters from people all over the world telling him that he was in their thoughts and wished him a speedy recovery. The most important letter he received, and the letter he discussed in his speech was from a white high school girl.[22] He used this letter to tell his audience that his misfortune was a signal to continue the fight. It was an example to King of the compassion that America did possess from black and white Americans, young and old. They were ready to move forward and change society.

Throughout this speech, King preached about the importance of the sit-in movement that took place in the early 1960s and how those sit-ins provided momentum and emotion to continue the struggle for racial equality. King demanded his audience understand that what people were fighting for was the protection of basic civil liberties. They fought to make sure that all American citizens had the rights that the Declaration of Independence and Constitution had forged, the right to live as free human beings in a free society. Like John F. Kennedy said in the civil rights speech, King also used the founding fathers as a symbolic point in his speech. It was the founding fathers that had forged the nation, and it was these men that should be used as an example of why the United States of America must be a country of equality and united not through superiority and separation. Yet, while King gave this speech of hope and wisdom he had no idea that the death bell had already begun to ring.

The major reason speeches are so amazing has to do with the poetic irony that they can convey. When King stood in front of the podium that evening, he had no idea that the very next day he would be gunned down by the very violence and indifference he sought to end. He discussed in his lecture, how happy he was with his life and that he would love to live a life of "longevity."[23] Looking at this fact in hindsight it can create an emotional surge, knowing that his life was going to be extremely short, lasting not even twenty-four hours more.

King was an excellent speaker and knew how to captivate an audience and rouse the emotions of his crowd. In the end, his message becomes a piece of poetic irony. On April 4, 1968, Martin Luther King Jr. was shot at the Lorraine Motel in Memphis, Tennessee by James Earl Ray.[24] With his death ended one era of the civil rights movement and thereafter the non-violent approach that King had tried so hard to secure, broke down and gave way to a much more aggressive approach epitomized by the Black Power movement and Black Panther Party. Although these movements and organizations had formed and been practicing their methods during Kings life, after his death they grew stronger with the growing need to gain black acceptance through black separation.

On the same evening that King was assassinated in Memphis trying to bring rights to black sanitation workers, Robert Kennedy took to the podium to tell his audience, mostly African American, the terrible news of the unnecessary tragedy. He did this as he was in the midst of his campaign to run for president in 1968. He wanted to discuss with the audience at the event the need, as a nation, to move forward. He spoke in Indianapolis, Indiana and what was supposed to be a campaign rally turned into an impromptu eulogy for the lost civil rights leader, one whom the audience saw as their hero.

When Kennedy stood in front of the audience they were in a positive mood and anticipating what Kennedy was going to say about his bid for the Democratic nomination. He looked at all of them, aware of the tragedy that they knew nothing about, and spoke to them from the heart. He discussed,

> Ladies and Gentlemen—I'm only going to talk to you just for a minute or so this evening. Because . . . I have some very sad news for all of you, and I think sad news for all of our fellow citizens, and people who love peace all over the world, and that is that Martin Luther King was shot and was killed tonight in Memphis, Tennessee.[25]

One can only begin to imagine the sorrow and heartache that must have been gripping the emotions of the audience, and everyone that was listening to his words. For Kennedy to be the person breaking this news to a huge audience, the anxiety must have been intense. He continued,

Martin Luther King dedicated his life to love and to justice between fellow human beings. He died in the cause of that effort. In this difficult day, in this difficult time for the United States, it's perhaps well to ask what kind of a nation we are and what direction we want to move in.[26]

Kennedy tried to soften his audience's sadness by telling them that King had died in an effort to secure the cause of human liberty.

Robert Kennedy then asked the shocked crowd to think about the type of country that they lived in and what direction the country ought to move towards without King as a part of it. In that same sense, Kennedy knew that sadness would give way to emptiness and that everyone would be filled with hatred, as well as the desire to avenge the death of their fallen leader. He continued,

> For those of you who are black—considering the evidence evidently is that there were white people who were responsible—you can be filled with bitterness, and with hatred, and a desire for revenge.[27]

As acknowledged in his speech, Kennedy believed that the perpetrator of the crime would likely be a white individual with a vendetta against King because of King's message. In the end, Kennedy was correct. When Kennedy gave the speech to his audience he did not know that in factuality. Even so, that did not stop him from telling his audience that he felt the crime was the work of a white man. He could have easily have lied to them and said this might be the work of an angry black citizen, but Kennedy's message must include his actual feelings if he was to make his point stick.

Kennedy told his audience that they could feel angry, be filled with hatred and want revenge, but they must only be allowed to possess the feelings, not act on them. He continued,

> We can move in that direction as a country, in greater polarization—black people amongst blacks, and white amongst whites, filled with hatred toward one another. Or we can make an effort, as Martin Luther King did, to understand and to comprehend, and replace that violence, that stain of bloodshed that has spread across our land, with an effort to understand, compassion and love.[28]

As Kennedy told those in the crowd, people can very easily separate themselves and join a common race against the other in this time of sorrow or live by the example that King died for. Forgo the need for violence and replace it with compassion and understanding among men. Society too easily allows itself to be overcome with the want to avenge its feelings of sorrow and loss. Too often society takes the wrong path with its policies and actions, and has failed to possess the moral leadership this country demands and requires. As Robert Kennedy told everyone, it was a necessity not a suggestion that people act in accordance with Martin Luther King's example and lead rather than follow.

Arguably, Robert Kennedy knew this would be a difficult task to ask them to accept. It is either plead for them to use civility or allow for the country to fall victim to severe violence. As a man running to become president, he asked for cooler heads to prevail. He stated,

> For those of you who are black and are tempted to be filled with hatred and mistrust of the injustice of such an act, against all white people, I would only say that I can also feel in my own heart the same kind of feeling. I had a member of my family killed, but he was killed by a white man.[29]

Robert Kennedy tried to connect with his audience on the same issue of loss. He reminded them of how his brother was killed by the same violence. He did this in order to redirect the target of their anger and shift their vengeance not toward the white race, but instead remind them that violence is color blind. The bull does not attack the flag because it is red. He attacks it because it is there. The violence committed in the name of revenge becomes part of the problem not a part of the solution. In another speech, at the University of California, Berkeley in 1966, Robert Kennedy alluded to this same idea. He stated that society knows now that,

> The color of an executioner's robe matters little. And we know in our hearts, even through time of passion and discontent, that to add to the quantity of violence is this country is to burden our own lives and mortgage our children's souls, and the best possibilities of the American future.[30]

Whether the killer was black or white mattered little to Kennedy. It was the action that should be examined. An act of violence killed an incredible human who was important to many people.

Kennedy, it seems, knew that the use of violence as a weapon of anger would not solve the problem they were faced with. Rather, it would eventually create a greater problem. If society does this it destroys the lives of its citizens and the potential of its children. Thus the very future of America is in jeopardy. All of this America can lose if violence is used out of hatred and revenge. As Kennedy stated,

> But we have to make an effort in the United States; we have to make an effort to understand, to get beyond these rather difficult times. My favorite poet was Aeschylus. He once wrote: 'Even in our sleep, pain which cannot forget falls drop by drop upon the heart, until, in our own despair, against our will, comes wisdom through the awful grace of God.'[31]

Kennedy, with all hope and sincerity, tried to erase his listeners need for open revenge with words that have in times of pain comforted him. He knew that his words and poetry would not ease the pains that they felt. Instead, people must make an effort to move forward. Instead of using revenge as a tool to ease the pain from this horror, people could use peace as an instrument to create a better society for all. If this was done, the type of pain they felt need not be felt again. Kennedy continued,

> What we need in the United States is not division; what we need in the United States is not hatred; what we need in the United States is not violence and lawlessness, but is love and wisdom, and compassion toward one another, and a feeling of justice toward those who still suffer within our country, whether they be white or whether they be black.[32]

As Kennedy reiterated, the country, at this time of mourning, did not need further separation between the races, nor violence, nor hatred, but rather the opposite of all of these things. Union, compassion, and understanding, the very dream King died for, was the mission they must join to complete. All races suffer violence and injustice, so more violence cannot be the answer.

What good does more violence accomplish? It does no good, only creates more fear, more pain, and more suffering. Kennedy went on,

> We can do well in this country. We will have difficult times. We've had difficult times in the past. And we will have difficult times in the future. It is not the end of violence; it is not the end of lawlessness; and it's not the end of disorder.[33]

Robert Kennedy tried, with an air of dignity and grace, to provide comfort in the most terrible of circumstances. He was there to provide a speech about supporting him in his run for the presidency, and instead found himself trying to console a nation. Hoping to understand and remember what King lived for, Kennedy hoped for everyone to realize that times have been difficult to tolerate in the past. He told them that the violence would not end with King's death, or the pain that was felt at that moment. Kennedy's message that night was that there was a need to be peaceful rather than violent. As he indicated, this task would be difficult and society must prepare for its inaction.

As Robert Kennedy finished his speech he provided advice through philosophy and hope. He stated,

> Let us dedicate ourselves to what the Greeks wrote so many years ago: to tame the savageness of man and make gentle the life of this world. Let us dedicate ourselves to that, and say a prayer for our country and for our people. Thank you very much.[34]

Kennedy's plea for a non-violent approach to the tragedy would seemingly fall on deaf ears as in the following days and weeks riots would erupt all over the country in response to the loss of King. From April 4 to April 8, 1968, riots broke out in Washington D.C, and would spread to one hundred ten United States cities, only Indianapolis, Indiana, where Kennedy spoke to a grieving audience, would not erupt into turmoil. The riots, especially in the District of Columbia, devastated the economic well being of the city. The destruction that took place caused hundred of businesses to close, people lost jobs, and insurance rates soared to unprecedented levels. Many people in the city, fearing the level of violence would grow even greater, left for the suburbs. The crime level gradually increased in the wake of the riots and soon discouraged investment in American cities. Economically the District of Columbia did not get back on track in some areas until 1991, and even 1999. As one can see, the hope that Robert Kennedy had for a peaceful retreat in the wake of such a profound death was not adhered to and as he warned the use of violence to combat violence caused serious problems for the country. As he said, violence met with violence does not solve any problems only makes the nation suffer from the effects longer.

With the leaders of change like John Kennedy, King and even Malcolm X departed, there was no symbol for black equality. The one person left that embodied this same sense of inspiration and understanding was the individual that spoke so eloquently about the passing of Martin Luther King, Robert Kennedy. He had been the younger brother of the late president, the Attorney General, and the Democratic Senator from New York. For many, Robert Kennedy was the last hope to salvage 1968 and the 1960s and stop the decade's unfortunate societal downfall. He was the vision of a new generation and the type of person people wanted to have sitting in the nation's highest elected position. On his shoulders rested the return of "Camelot," racial equality, help for the poor, and a return of America's true objective to help those that could not help their own security.

On April 5, 1968, Robert F. Kennedy would again take to the stage to speak to an audience of faithful listeners. He wanted his audience to come to the realization that America had serious problems and these concerns needed to be repaired. His main objective was to discuss the issue of violence in American society. He wanted to talk to his audience about this growing threat to peace in America and around the globe. He offered no incredible ways to fix the issues plaguing the country, but rather offered the audience an outline of the severity of the situation. In so doing, he asked them to move forward and provide future generations with the information needed to begin the journey to stop what he labeled the "Mindless Menace of Violence."

This speech is the backdrop of this work. By understanding Robert Kennedy's words on violence, society can appreciate that things can change. It is a speech that goes relatively unnoticed and is not listed in the leading works dedicated to the most profound speeches in American history. In reality, it is a speech that has passed the test of time and can be used as a beacon of hope for past generations, this generation, and future generations. Kennedy's speech on violence attempted to discuss the problem of violence in America, some of the reasons it had taken hold on American soil, and the knowledge that in order to stop the useless bloodshed in America it will be a long and arduous fight. What he was saying can be used to discuss civil rights riots, gang violence, and in today's society, school shootings. The message he attempted to convey was and is still clear. The taking of another person's life, for whatever reason, is wrong and violence will only be met in the end with more violence. Still, as he discussed, American society has refused to act and in great measure has allowed for the violence to continue.

In the final analysis, Kennedy's words that he presented at the City Club of Cleveland in Cleveland, Ohio on April 5, 1968, are etched in history not only as a reminder of the violence that has gripped the United States throughout its history, but rather an indication as to what will happen if nothing is done to stop it. It is also a reflection of the hope and belief that things can change and life can be less violent. That is if at least one person is willing to say "enough is enough." Since the 1960s, society has progressed in many unbelievable ways and civilization itself has changed its moral stance on many major issues, but still issues are left unchecked. When students can go to school and shoot their fellow students whether it is in an elementary school, a high school, or a college campus, the nation is damaged, because the level of violence has yet to be pushed back. Too many times people in this country and other counties will say, "What can I do? Violence has always been around and it is human nature." Correct, violence has always tainted the canvas of history and society, not only in America but in the world. Therefore, this author sets out to challenge everyone in the world with a task. Try to change!

In the long history of the world, there have been instances when one person stood up against what they perceived as the immoral or illegal actions of society. There was a time when slavery was viewed by the majority as acceptable and incapable of change. Still there were many who strove to make a difference and work towards its eternal abolition. William Wilberforce, a man that dedicated his life to the abolition of slavery and the international slave trade in Great Britain, is the type of person that worked to promote change. He was a man that was scorned, ridiculed, and mentally abused, yet he moved forward in the face of powerful opposition. As Benjamin Hughes said of William Wilberforce,

> I present you no bloodstained hero; he has led no slaughtering armies, he has desolated no kingdoms; for him no triumphal arch is reared; his laurels have

been won in another and nobler sphere. He was no aspirant to popular applause; no time serving politician; he was the friend of the 'robbed and peeled;' [and] emphatically one of the greatest men of modern time . . . the Hercules of Abolition.[35]

Wilberforce felt that slavery was wrong, even when people disagreed and friends would not support him. Yet still he moved forward building support in the British Empire to end the institution of slavery. Days before Wilberforce was to die of a long time illness, he succeeded in helping abolish slavery in Great Britain. Wilberforce had succeeded in eradicating an institution that many at one point viewed as indestructible, as necessary, and as human nature would allow. His vision became the moral beacon and an example of how one man can change the course of human events.

If points of view can change, people can change, ambitions can change, therefore it is only right to believe that society can change and therefore human nature can change. People do not have to live in a world where they are fearful, or live in a society where they have to accept the intangible level of violence that is around them. Of course this is not a problem that can be cured over night, and it is not suggested that this is a problem that will be fixed in this generation or even with the next generation. Rather, this is a suggestion for society to finally stand up and say "enough is enough." The world will never change if people do nothing, but there is always the possibility of change when at least one person makes that attempt. I may only speak for myself, but a world in which people try, rather than use excuses sounds like a great place to live. That is why the speech given by Robert Kennedy on the "Mindless Menace of Violence" is so important to our generation's understanding of the past, as well as a message to help us in creating the future. People need to realize that the blueprints required to build a lasting future have already been written and the point of history is not to allow it to repeat itself. Through Kennedy's words society will not repeat past mistakes. Instead people will work to create a better world for all to live in.

Robert Kennedy's speech delivered in one of the most tumultuous years in American history, 1968, carried a message that survived its own time and has now lived into our own. In today's society, Kennedy's message rings louder and stronger than it has ever before. One must look at his writing and hear his speech and be reminded of what America is, has been, and can be. Even so, this same understanding cannot be realized until America is free of this terrible and senseless chain of bloodshed. Each and every American has the right to live. Using violence to take away someone's right to their own life is the grossest act of terror. Even with his words of wisdom for the future and the battle to conquer violence, Kennedy, just like his brother and Martin Luther King Jr., would also fall victim to irony and was gunned down by an assassin. The very violence they sought to remedy ended his life.

On June 5, 1968, two months to the day of the "Mindless Menace of Violence" speech, Robert Kennedy was assassinated by Sirhan Sirhan at the Ambassador Hotel in California as he thanked countless supporters for their help in bringing him a victory in the California primary. Like King, the path for Robert Kennedy was short and ended again with the American flag at half staff. His own words then became a reminder not only of the violence staining America, but served as a reminder of the cost of trying to create a better society for all. Robert Kennedy was laid to rest in Arlington National Cemetery in Arlington, Virginia. Although it had always been his wish to be buried in Massachusetts, his family found it appropriate to bury him closer to his brother.

Robert and John Kennedy were men unfortunately living the sad tale of irony, inspired by their devotion to stopping senseless violence. What could they have done for America? This is a question interesting to ponder, but in the end nothing more than speculation and assumptions. In the coming pages, Robert Kennedy's "Mindless Menace of Violence" speech will be examined. With each passage the message of his words will be provided and in so doing the reader will look at the connection of his words to the country that has been created since they were written. Through his speech, an examination of the problem of violence will be discussed as will events of our past and present that have come to convey the very impact of violence and indifference he warned the country about.

The spoken word and speeches presented throughout history are a fantastic source, providing future generations a medium by which to use in looking into the past for answers to the future. The "Mindless Menace of Violence" speech holds the key to societies most pressing issue's today. Even so, there are many speeches from the past that provide and present inspiration to future generation and the reasons for this are endless. They too will be examined and provided to shed light on the history of America, and also the history of those that used words to stir emotion. These types of speeches show the power that a few people in our American past offered to the study of history and the understanding of our American identity. Whether an individual today believes it or not, one person can change the course of history, even if only with words of encouragement. Can a speech provided by Robert Kennedy on "violence" or Martin Luther King Jr. on his "dreams" help make people feel better with all the tragedies still being perpetrated on American soil? The words of these speeches speak for themselves, therefore beginning our study of the "Mindless Menace of Violence" speech. Kennedy stood in front of a large audience in Cleveland and spoke the following words,

This is a time of shame and sorrow. It is not a day for politics. I have saved this one opportunity, my only event of today, to speak briefly to you about the mindless menace of violence in America which again stains our land and every one of our lives.

It is not the concern of any one race. The victims of the violence are black and white, rich and poor, young and old, famous and unknown. They are, most important of all, human beings whom other human beings loved and needed. No one—no matter where he lives or what he does—can be certain who will suffer from some senseless act of bloodshed. And yet it goes on and on and on in this country of ours.

Why? What has violence ever accomplished? What has it ever created? No martyr's cause has ever been stilled by an assassin's bullet. No wrongs have ever been righted by riots and civil disorders. A sniper is only a coward, not a hero; and an uncontrolled, uncontrollable mob is only the voice of madness, not the voice of reason.

Whenever any American's life is taken by another American unnecessarily— whether it is done in the name of the law or in the defiance of the law, by one man or a gang, in cold blood or in passion, in an attack of violence or in response to violence—whenever we tear at the fabric of the life which another man has painfully and clumsily woven for himself and his children, the whole nation is degraded.

'Among free men,' said Abraham Lincoln, 'there can be no successful appeal from the ballot to the bullet; and those who take such appeal are sure to lose their cause and pay the costs.'

Yet we seemingly tolerate a rising level of violence that ignores our common humanity and our claims to civilization alike. We calmly accept newspaper reports of civilian slaughter in far-off lands. We glorify killing on movie and television screens and call it entertainment. We make it easy for men of all shades of sanity to acquire whatever weapons and ammunition they desire.

Too often we honor swagger and bluster and wielders of force; too often we excuse those who are willing to build their own lives on the shattered dreams of others. Some Americans who preach non-violence abroad fail to practice it here at home. Some who accuse others of inciting riots have by their own conduct invited them.

Some look for scapegoats, others look for conspiracies, but this much is clear: violence breeds violence, repression brings retaliation, and only a cleansing of our whole society can remove this sickness from our soul.

For there is another kind of violence, slower but just as deadly destructive as the shot or the bomb in the night. This is the violence of institutions; indifference and inaction and slow decay. This is the violence that afflicts the poor, that poisons relations between men because their skin has different colors. This is the slow destruction of a child by hunger, and schools without books and homes without heat in the winter.

This is the breaking of a man's spirit by denying him the chance to stand as a father and as a man among other men. And this too afflicts us all.

I have not come here to propose a set of specific remedies nor is there a single set. For a broad and adequate outline we know what must be done. When you teach a man to hate and fear his brother, when you teach that he is a lesser man because of his color or his beliefs or the policies he pursues, when you teach that those who differ from you threaten your freedom or your job or your family, then you also learn to confront others not as fellow citizens but as ene-

mies, to be met not with cooperation but with conquest; to be subjugated and mastered.

We learn, at the last, to look at our brothers as aliens, men with whom we share a city, but not a community; men bound to us in common dwelling, but not in common effort. We learn to share only a common fear, only a common desire to retreat from each other, only a common impulse to meet disagreement with force. For all this, there are no final answers.

Yet we know what we must do. It is to achieve true justice among our fellow citizens. The question is not what programs we should seek to enact. The question is whether we can find in our own midst and in our own hearts that leadership of humane purpose that will recognize the terrible truths of our existence.

We must admit the vanity of our false distinctions among men and learn to find our own advancement in the search for the advancement of others. We must admit in ourselves that our own children's future cannot be built on the misfortunes of others. We must recognize that this short life can neither be ennobled or enriched by hatred or revenge.

Our lives on this planet are too short and the work to be done too great to let this spirit flourish any longer in our land. Of course we cannot vanquish it with a program, nor with a resolution.

But we can perhaps remember, if only for a time, that those who live with us are our brothers, that they share with us the same short moment of life; that they seek, as do we, nothing but the chance to live out their lives in purpose and in happiness, winning what satisfaction and fulfillment they can.

Surely, this bond of common faith, this bond of common goal, can begin to teach us something. Surely, we can learn, at least, to look at those around us as fellow men, and surely we can begin to work a little harder to bind up the wounds among us and to become in our own hearts brothers and countrymen once again.

NOTES

1. Norman L. Rosenberg, *In Our Times: America since World War II* (New Jersey: Prentice Hall, 2003), 120-123.

2. Rosenberg, 118-120.

3. William H. Chafe, *The Unfinished Journey: America Since World War II* (New York: Oxford University Press, 2003), 213-214.

4. Philip A. Klinkner, *The Unsteady March: The Rise and Decline of Racial Equality in America* (Chicago: The University of Chicago Press, 1999), 264-265.

5. Klinkner, 264-265.

6. Klinkner, 264-265.

7. Klinkner, 267.

8. John F. Kennedy, "Special Message to the Congress on Civil Rights and Job Opportunities," (Televised address to the American people from oval office in the White House in Washington, D.C. on 19 June 1963), Public Papers, John F. Kennedy Library, Boston, MA. 483.

9. Kennedy, "Special Message to the Congress," 19 June 1963, 483.

10. Kennedy, "Special Message to the Congress," 19 June 1963, 483.

11. Kennedy, "Special Message to the Congress," 19 June 1963, 483.

12. Kennedy, "Special Message to the Congress," 19 June 1963, 483.

13. Chafe, 225-226, 229.

14. Chafe, 355-356.

15. Chafe, 355.

16. Martin Luther King Jr., "Mountaintop Speech," (Sermon delivered at the Mason Temple, the World Headquarters for the Church of God in Christ, located in Memphis, Tennessee on 3 April 1968. One night before Dr. King was assassinated). Transcript of speech is located at the Estate of Dr. Martin Luther King Jr. in Atlanta, Georgia.

17. King, "I've Seen the Promised Land," 3 April 1968.

18. Albert Camus, *Quotes*, 2008.

19. King, "I've Seen the Promised Land," 3 April 1968.

20. Albert Camus, *Quotes*, 2008.

21. King, "I've Seen the Promised Land," 3 April 1968.

22. King, "I've Seen the Promised Land," 3 April 1968.

23. King, "I've Seen the Promised Land," 3 April 1968.

24. Terry H. Anderson, *The Sixties*. (Boston: Pearson Longman, 2007), 105-106.

25. Robert F. Kennedy, "On the Death of Reverend Dr. Martin Luther King Jr.," (Speech delivered regarding Death of Dr. Martin Luther King Jr. from Indianapolis, Indiana on 4 April 1968). Robert F. Kennedy Senate Files Archive in the John F. Kennedy Library, part of the National Archives.

26. Kennedy, "On the Death of Reverend Dr. Martin Luther King Jr.," 4 April 1968.

27. Kennedy, "On the Death of Reverend Dr. Martin Luther King Jr.," 4 April 1968.

28. Kennedy, "On the Death of Reverend Dr. Martin Luther King Jr.," 4 April 1968.

29. Kennedy, "On the Death of Reverend Dr. Martin Luther King Jr.," 4 April 1968.

30. Robert F. Kennedy, "The Color of an Executioner's Robe Matters Little," (Anti-war speech given at the University of California, Berkeley on 22 October 1966). Robert F. Kennedy Senate Files Archive in the John F. Kennedy Library, part of the National Archives.

31. Kennedy, "On the Death of Reverend Dr. Martin Luther King Jr.," 4 April 1968.

32. Kennedy, "On the Death of Reverend Dr. Martin Luther King Jr.," 4 April 1968.

33. Kennedy, "On the Death of Reverend Dr. Martin Luther King Jr.," 4 April 1968.

34. Kennedy, "On the Death of Reverend Dr. Martin Luther King Jr.," 4 April 1968.

35. Kevin Belmonte, *William Wilberforce: A Hero for Humanity* (Michigan: Zondervan, 2007, 16.

Chapter Two

The Victims of Violence

At the Olympic Games it is not the finest and the strongest men who are crowned, but they who enter the lists . . . So, too, in the life of the honorable and the good it is they who act rightly who win the prize.

—Aristotle

When I was a child, I found myself always intrigued by history and the study of the past. Whether I was learning about Ancient Rome, Egyptian history, and any aspect of American history, I found myself engulfed in the world I was studying. Most captivating about the past was the level of sorrow and happiness that was present in these major events in world history. There seemed to be a great moment and a tragic moment for every event that I studied. Rome was able to create an empire, but it eventually collapsed under the rule of atrocious leaders overcome by their own thoughts of invincibility. Yet, still while one looks at American history they see glory and sorrow. The wars that were won, the people that have died, it is a history that evokes patriotism and sadness. I have devoted my life to the study of the American past because I believe that it is a wonderful history and that this nation has a valuable place to occupy in the history of civilization. Still, this nation has made mistakes, and it must be held accountable for them. The point of history is not to bash a nation for its mistakes, but rather to learn from them and move on creating a nation free from falling victim to the same mishaps. Society uses the past to tell people who they are and what they are meant to become. I love reading about John Adams or Andrew Jackson, learning about the promise of their endeavors yet understanding the miscalculations of their times. Use them as examples of how to learn from their mistakes and praise their achievements. Whether in Jackson's case to learn of the oppression of Native Americans and the ushering in of an era of common man politics or in Adams' case the ability to keep a growing nation from crumbling apart yet diminishing several civil liberties society must always protect. Through their experiences society seeks to understand the people that helped form the democratic principles of this nation. History is the ability to learn why the nation I have come to love is the way it is, good and bad. That is history for me.

When I think of something ironic in the historical sense, it means that I read about something occurring or being said, and then soon after the same issue that was being addressed is the cause of more pain. This can be seen in the discussion of the deaths of Martin Luther King Jr. and Robert F. Kennedy. When King was assassinated the day after his "Mountaintop" sermon and Robert Kennedy killed two months to the day after his "Mindless Menace of Violence" speech, these are incidents that would fall under the category of historical irony. It is because what the speeches that these men presented were designed to combat and tackle were at the very heart of violence in American society.

On April 5, 1968, one day after the assassination of Martin Luther King, Robert Kennedy spoke to a group of listeners about violence in America. This chapter will deal with the first quarter of his speech. Therefore, the most important way to analyze and critique this work for meaning and understanding is to examine this speech and discuss the circumstances surrounding the words Kennedy chose to use that evening. In the first paragraph of the speech, Kennedy sets the tone of the entire speech. He commented,

This is a time of shame and sorrow. It is not a day for politics. I have saved this one opportunity, my only event of today, to speak briefly to you about the mindless menace of violence in America which again stains our land and every one of our lives.

Robert Kennedy seemed to have understood that the words he chose to utter would be analyzed and discussed for decades, after all this was the day after Martin Luther King Jr. had been brutally killed by none other than an assassin with a high powered rifle. The type of pain that Kennedy spoke of was not unusual and he had felt it before. In the past this pain had changed his outlook on life. Now he saw a perfect opportunity to use his experience and understanding to change the country, which was beginning to be consumed by the very violence that destroyed all good things the nation had created.

Robert Kennedy began his speech by telling his audience that he was angered and disappointed at society for forcing him to pay witness to another terrible act of senseless violence. Kennedy felt that in the long scheme of things, politics was the part that individuals play in helping to create a better world and using the political arena to protect those that are at risk. In that same argument, politics must not be thought of as life or death, but rather a development and a process which must acknowledge tragedy. Therefore, the wheels of the political spectrum must stop to pay homage and recognize the life of a fallen leader, as the nation itself mourned and tried to make sense of their surroundings. Robert Kennedy at this point in history was in the middle of a presidential campaign, and attempting to capitalize on his popularity to become the Democratic nominee.

It was understood that Robert Kennedy had been in this type of position before, although much more personal, having served as Attorney General of the United States when the same type of senseless violence had taken his brother. If anyone had the knowledge or strength to discuss violence after the assassination of another political leader, it was him. In his speech Kennedy makes the point to tell his crowd that he has "saved this one opportunity, my only event of today" to speak to the crowd about his feelings on the tragedy that had transpired. Kennedy reserved this one time on April 5th to discuss his hopes as a citizen of America, citizen of the world and a man made of flesh and bone wishing to live his life in happiness and in safety. He addressed the crowd as a man fearful of his own well-being, afraid for his family's safety, and terrified about the future of the country he loved.

In Kennedy's eyes, violence had been one of the countries greatest blemishes on its reputation. He had seen the level of violence grow at an unparalleled rate in American history and now was beginning to realize that there was developing a new surge of violence, which endangered the very existence of the country and tarnished its very image. With a growing level of violence swiftly taking hold, the lives of all Americans began to be smeared and the great majority of citizens came to the realization that in America, if political leaders can be killed at random so can anyone else. If violence is allowed to continue there is no telling where the country's future can end up. In a country overcome by violence can anyone live the life they have the right to live? Kennedy began his speech with the need to express that America had been stained, and that could not change. What is done is done, and the past cannot be altered. But, in that same expression, Kennedy believed that although one could be inflicted with a stain, one could also wash it away. The first thing that must be done to wash away the violence that is destroying America is to recognize that it is there. If society blindly moves forward unaware or unwilling to recognize the blemish on or around us, it will forever remain. Yet, if Americans recognize it, understand its origin, and quickly move to remedy it, they can succeed in reversing the course of events and come out on the other side.

Kennedy continued his speech by telling the American people that the issue at hand was not an issue of race, nor the concern of any one race. Rather the issue of violence, which had waged war on American society, was an issue that had trickled past the color barrier and seeped into every corner of American society. His position was that,

> *It is not the concern of any one race. The victims of the violence are black and white, rich and poor, young and old, famous and unknown. They are, most important of all, human beings whom other human beings loved and needed. No one—no matter where he lives or what he does—can be certain who will suffer from some senseless act of bloodshed. And yet it goes on and on and on in this country of ours.*

By conveying to the audience that the victims of violence were "black and white" Kennedy attempted to show that both races were equal in the eyes of violence and that any race was susceptible to the anguish, which violence always inflicts. Showing that the victims were "rich and poor" allowed Kennedy to reach out to every type of American, no matter their class standing. In so doing, he could identify with every citizen in America and explain to them that no one in the world was safe from that type of aggression. Even though they may escape the initial fire caused by the violence around them, anyone can be subjected to the smoke over their heads. For the attack of violence is not the only worry in a free society, it is just the most visible. The unforeseen danger lies in the destruction of families from tragic and untimely deaths, collapse of a nation's image through unwarranted war, and the apathy of a citizenry overcome and burdened by fear. Violence need not burn someone to be able to harm them. That Kennedy understood then and a fact our society must acknowledge today.

Violence does not care if the victim is young or old, known or unknown. John F. Kennedy became a victim of violence, a man of wealth, fame and status, but in contrast, a six year old girl by the name of Kayla Rolland who was shot and killed at Buell Elementary School near Flint, Michigan on February 29, 2000, can also become a victim of this terrible violence. Her attacker was identified as a six year old boy that was a classmate and brought a .32-caliber handgun to school. Kayla would die from her wounds as Kennedy from his. They were the victims of violence. Robert Kennedy was determined to explain that in American society it was violence that was the enemy not each other. Violence is a tool of hatred. To hate is to become full of fear and anger and when the level has risen to a boiling point, the individual in question will explode with rage and use the tool of violence to cause pain on those they encounter. Therefore society must address the issue of violence and those that use it as an instrument of expression. But, as Kennedy discussed and asked for everyone to understand, the victims of violence can be anyone.

Although the events surrounding the deaths of President Kennedy and Kayla Rolland may appear to have nothing to do with one another, they are in their spirit the type of violence that Robert Kennedy was trying to bring awareness to. One need only look to our present generation for more instances of violence that seem so chaotic and unexplainable. On March 24, 1998 four students and one teacher were killed and ten others wounded outside Westside Middle School in Jonesboro, Arkansas as it was being emptied during a false fire alarm. Mitchell Johnson, 13, and Andrew Golden, 11, sat in the woods and shot at their classmates and teachers as they came outside from the school.[1] On October 3, 2006, 32-year-old Charles Carl Roberts IV entered the one-room West Nickel Mines Amish School and shot ten schoolgirls, ranging in age from six to thirteen, and then turned the gun on himself. Five of the girls and Roberts died.[2]

These events are the type of violence that Robert Kennedy warned the country about. The victims of violence can be anyone and in today's society it is our schools that are the most susceptible to this type of bloodshed. Most importantly, Kennedy also showed that no matter who was killed, in the end they were human beings whom other human beings loved and cherished. Everyone is mortal. Each one of those girls that were shot at the Amish school had families and with their passing their families are left to grieve. Sadly their parents and loved ones are left in sorrow, wondering what could have been if only their child had not attended school that day. In that same respect, Robert Kennedy states that "No one—no matter where he lives or what he does—can be certain who will suffer from some senseless act of bloodshed." What if Kayla had stayed home sick from school that day? Then today she might be alive and would not have fell victim to a senseless act of violence in another American school.

Looking back on these events in hindsight no one can know when a senseless act of violence will again stain our land. These types of acts are also directly linked to hate. As seen recently, "Ten years after Wyoming College student Matthew Shepard was brutally murdered because of his sexual orientation, a fifteen year old gay California student" was killed after a fellow student "shot him because of his sexual orientation and gender expression." The student, identified as Lawrence King, was an eighth-grader at E.O. Junior High School in Oxnard and was shot by a fourteen year old attacker who was "among a group of students known to bully and harass King because he sometimes wore makeup and jewelry and told classmates he was gay."[3] The attacker is to be charged with murder and a hate crime. This was another example of the level of violence which has inflicted pain on our society. Whether someone is gay or straight, black or white, rich or poor, should not be a reason to look at them differently or with any hatred or suspicion.

Everyone in this nation has the right to live their lives in happiness and satisfaction and choose to live the life they wish. No one has the right to destroy the very dream one person has created, because they disagree or see a lifestyle as immoral. I have always grown up respectful of people for who they are and what they chose to do with their life. If someone in America just so happens to be born gay or questions their gender identity, who am I to hate them or disagree with them for the life they are living. If a man wishes to marry another man, or a woman desires to marry another woman, why should our society deny their feelings to want to live their lives in happiness? Their life and choice to marry will not affect any choice that I make. It seems rather unacceptable for some to tell others that they may not enjoy the rights of marriage because they love a member of the same sex. Therefore I pose a question, how would a heterosexual couple feel if they were told they could not get married and enjoy equal rights under the law? It seems deplorable for a society and government to deny same sex couples equal rights under the law. They are human beings that love and are loved and therefore entitled to human rights, which they so clearly are being denied in America. To date, only Massachusetts and California have taken court action and legalized gay marriage, a major step in the right direction for the civil rights of gay couples.

The question of sexual orientation is a major issue in American society and can find itself in many cases of violence that have occurred in America. But, as mentioned before, the victims of violence take many shapes, many forms, and my connotations. The victims of violence are everywhere. When one looks at events in the past he or she may wish things could have transpired differently. This can be said for Cassie Bernall, 17, Steven Curnow, 14, Corey DePotter, 17, Kelly Fleming, 16, Matthew Kechter, 16, Dan Mouser, 15, Daniel Rohrbough, 15, Rachel Scott, 17, Isaiah Shoels, 18, John Tomlin, 16, Lauren Townsend, 18, and Kyle Valasquez, 16, all of whom became victims of the growing school violence that stains American society. Each student went to school believing that they were in a safe environment and each ready to show the world the product of their ambitions, yet each student became embroiled in an issue that has yet to be defeated. This was not theirs or anyone else's fault. Blame resides on the ones that carried out the carnage. These were the victims of the Columbine Massacre and when America cries over the violence in society and in our schools, they remember the hope that was lost. Our goal as fellow human beings should be to help move forward in society and to eradicate the sorrow that afflicts family and friends. A society that allows for this type of violence to go unchecked is a society out of touch with its own people and with itself. This is the agony Robert Kennedy spoke of and the senseless bloodshed he feared would destroy American families. Yet, today our society moves forward unwilling to challenge the level of violence which destroys families.

Just recently, another school shooting brought tears to many more young people and brought a country again to its knees in sorrow. On the college campus of Northern Illinois University a gunman by the name of Steve Kazmierczak, 27, walked into a lecture hall occupied by an estimated one hundred and sixty students and without saying a word opened fire.[4] Eighteen people would be injured before the gunman turned the gun on himself and allowed the chaos and violence to destroy him as well. In all, five students were killed during this brutal and unnecessary attack on another college campus where again students, who are our most important product, have become our most targeted commodity. Daniel Parmenter, 20, Catalina Garcia, 20, Ryanne Mace, 19, Julianna Gehant, 32 and Gayle Dubowski, 20 were killed during the attack. This tragedy was again a failure to recognize the words of warning that Kennedy had left future generations since 1968. He spoke of this horrible violence then and how if left unchecked our most important product, our youth, would become the greatest victim.

The power of the written word, especially speeches, is enormous. Speeches can provide a glimpse not only into the past but into the present as well. They can be used to discuss events that have just occurred and allow many to use them to make sense of the world. When Kennedy discussed that there was no way of telling when some senseless act of violence was going to be perpetrated again, it causes one to think about their well-being. Anyone could be caught in the same type of violence that someone else falls victim to. School teachers all over America understand that there is always the possibility that someone will try and copy the Columbine shooting. There is the possibility, like then, that a teacher could be killed for simply doing their job. William Dave Sanders, 47, was the only teacher killed in the Columbine shootings in 1999. He died protecting his students from a threat that never should have existed. It will soon be seen that even in the worst of moments mankind can find the most amazing abilities of human beings and their ability to provide compassion. Sanders gave his life for his students and in the end became a victim in 1999 of the violence that Kennedy spoke of in 1968, ironically almost thirty one years to the day that Kennedy ushered his warning on violence. Many college professors thought the same way after the Virginia Tech Massacre. Many watched these events transpire seeing that life is fragile. The destruction at North Illinois University is another example of the innocence that violence has consumed.

Sadly, on April 25, 2008 a man by the name of Eric Thompson spoke at Virginia Tech to students that were supporting an initiative to legally carry weapons to classrooms. They felt that if students were allowed to carry weapons to class then this type of attack would easily have been stopped. Not surprisingly, Eric Thompson is an online weapons dealer, based in Green Bay,

Wisconsin, and just so happened to have sold one of the guns to Seung-Hui Cho who massacred students and faculty at Virginia Tech and one of the guns to Steve Kazmierczak the shooter at Northern Illinois. He spoke at the college in favor of allowing students to bring weapons to school. It seems so surreal for people to truly think that the answer to gun violence is more guns. How could anyone feel safe in a classroom where dozens of students have guns? As a professor, I would never teach in a classroom that allows students to carry weapons. While they may have the freedom to possess weapons, I have the freedom to refuse to accept an incredible manipulation of tragedy. Those students died because gun control laws are inadequate, and one person was able to obtain a weapon through the internet. I think it is clear that the problem is not whether or not students were protected, but rather the ability of one to obtain weapons to harm others.

I remember being at a restaurant eating my lunch when I first heard the news report that there had been a shooting on the college campus of Virginia Tech. At first I was overcome with anger and then compassion for the victims and their families. It struck me as odd that again this massacre took place in April, which was the same month Columbine took place and ironically the same month that Kennedy had spoke about violence. I could not help but wonder if the school age rhyme of "April showers bring May flowers," would ever come true. So many Aprils, so much horror and still the level of violence had risen again. Still in today's society this level of hostility has consistently risen and more shootings in malls, schools, and businesses have begun to create a societal emotional breakdown. I think that the massacre at Virginia Tech affected me greatly when I heard about the heroic work of one of the teachers, Professor Liviu Librescu, a Holocaust survivor who had taught at Virginia Tech for twenty years. Here was a gentlemen that had lived through the greatest example of human indifference known to man and had survived.

On that fateful day, Professor Librescu used his body to block the classroom door, while allowing his students to escape the carnage around them. He died, ironically enough on Holocaust Remembrance Day, so that his students could live. This was a sad story, but another example of how in instances of pure terror, human nature shows its true potential. Human nature is good at heart and there are many who want to create a better world for all. Unfortunately, these same people that have dedicated their lives to their students or to their friends and family have found themselves on the front lines of our generation's greatest battle. This battle is not being waged in Iraq or part of America's "War on Terror." Rather our greatest struggle is the protection of the American ideal from the violence consistently strangling our nation's citizens. There is much to fear from outside our nation's borders in an age of growing terrorism, but there is more to dread from within our nation's boundaries. America must move forward, looking to curb the level of violence that is destroying our national will to live without fear. Society is beginning to believe that violence is normal and part of everyday life, but this attitude must change and our hope for the future must redirect its course.

Regrettably, Virginia Tech has become an example of American society's inability to uncover why these events take place and the lasting consequence of our inaction. The senseless bloodshed inflicted on the campus of Virginia Tech would leave the following individual's dreams shattered and their potential in American society unknown for eternity. They are Ross Alameddine, Jamie Bishop, Brian Bluhm, Ryan Clark, Austin Cloyd, Jocelyne Couture-Nowak, Kevin Granata, Matt Gwaltney, Caitlin Hammaren, Jeremy Herbstritt, Rachael Hill, Emily Hilscher, Matthew La Porte, Jarrett Lane, Henry Lee, Liviu Librescu, G.V. Loganathan, Partahi Mamora Halomoan Lumbantoruan, Lauren McCain, Daniel O'Neil, Juan Ramon Ortiz, Minal Panchal, Daniel Perez Cueva, Erin Peterson, Michael Pohle, Julia Pryde, Mary Read, Reema Samaha, Waleed Shaalan, Leslie G. Sherman, Maxine Turner, and Nicole Regina White. These are the victims of Virginia Tech and in a larger sense the victims of the raising level of violence in American society. So again, almost unknowingly society commits to its destruction, so that history again, does not repeat itself. Sadly, with the death of five young individuals at North Illinois University and one young student at a junior high in California, our ability to keep the senseless violence at bay can so far be considered a failure, but the battle wages on. The only certainty in the final analysis is that nothing will change if people do nothing. There are no absolute certainties when it comes to life and death. There is in that same understanding, something very sad that people are left without these certainties. Where are the feelings of security and how can our society make the wisdom of Robert Kennedy a reality?

Human beings have the right to life and the ability to live a fruitful one at that. Yet, the uncertainty in life does not come from whether one will get ill or die in a tragic accident. The terrible uncertainty comes from whether one person is willing to destroy another's life for the means of his or her own objectives. In this case, the issue of violence is the insecurity and the loss of life to this tragic vagueness and yet in American society this tragedy is unending. Robert Kennedy told his audience that this type of senseless bloodshed goes on and on in American society and that was in the 1960s. In the new millennium, this same type of violence still stains the American landscape and goes unchallenged. Innocent people still lose their lives to the lunatic rampage of others. Today, American society is still left sobbing for the loss of another innocent and again left wondering what inspiration that person could have provided the world if only they did not succumb to a violent act.

The question that Robert Kennedy pondered and which he asked the audience to think about was,

Why? What has violence ever accomplished? What has it ever created? No martyr's cause has ever been stilled by an assassin's bullet.

In the long history of the world has violence ever been successful? In this case, Kennedy was not discussing the violence of military combat, but rather the violence of society with no military objective. What Kennedy pondered and asked his audience to acknowledge, was that when an innocent person is killed in cold blood, no good comes of it. That person is gone, the gifts they could have bestowed on society are left unachieved and the killer is left to live with the cold fact that he is simply a killer. In some instances the perpetrator takes his own life in the aftermath of the carnage and his thoughts and reasons go unknown in the course of time. Kennedy keyed in on the fact that the violence that was on everyone's mind was the tragic death of Martin Luther King. Therefore Kennedy digressed for a moment to focus on the fact that the person that carried out the violence was an assassin.

Kennedy is also all too familiar with the idea of assassins. Lee Harvey Oswald had acted alone only five years prior in 1963, committing arguably one of the greatest murders in world history. In his heart the objective of that assassin was unsuccessful. Although Oswald killed the president, he failed to overthrow and destroy the existing government forcing the country into anarchy. The picture of Lyndon B. Johnson taking the oath of office on Air Force One, standing right next to the newly widowed Jacqueline Kennedy, has been engrained in people's minds, even if they did not live during this event. The picture itself although captivating, sad, and historic, carries with it a totally different meaning. The concept is renewal. Although the country had lost its leader, the institutions of the American government were left intact and therefore the government moved forward. A new president was sworn in and the country carried on its daily routine, all the while not forgetting the fallen leader.

So in that sense do assassins ever obtain the objective of their act? They take it upon themselves, whether alone or part of a conspiracy, to take part in a violent act aimed at a leading figure. American history has been marred by political assassinations to a level unmatched arguably by any other society or empire. On January 30, 1835, President Andrew Jackson went to the United States capitol to attend the funeral services of Congressman Warren R. Davis of South Carolina. As the President walked past the casket and began to move toward the capitol rotunda, Richard Lawrence, moved towards him, drew a pistol, and fired point blank at Jackson. The bullet failed to discharge from the gun barrel, and Jackson was unhurt. Jackson then lunged at Lawrence and lifted his cane above his head to beat the assailant for his act of violence. Before he could hit Lawrence with his cane, Lawrence drew a second pistol and fired again at the president. A second bang was heard, but again the gun failed to fire. The odds against both guns misfiring were extremely high.[5]

The thirty two year old Lawrence wanted to kill President Jackson because he claimed that Jackson had killed his father three years earlier. But Lawrence also claimed to be the rightful heir to the British throne, so his word was seen as that of a lunatic. Evidence then surfaced that Lawrence's father had been dead for twelve years and had never even visited America. A jury found Lawrence not guilty on grounds of insanity and he was hospitalized at the Washington Government Hospital for the Insane. He died twenty six years later.[6] The assassination attempt on Andrew Jackson was the first of its kind, but would not be the last.

Many people perceive America to be a country prone to political violence. Nine American presidents, Andrew Jackson in 1835, Abraham Lincoln in 1865, James Garfield in 1881, William McKinley in 1901, Harry S. Truman in 1950, John F. Kennedy in 1963, Richard Nixon in 1974, Gerald Ford twice in 1975, and Ronald Reagan in 1981, have been the targets of assassination.[7] In addition, eight governors, seven U.S. Senators, nine U.S. Congressmen, eleven mayors, seventeen state legislators, and eleven judges have been violently attacked. No other country with a population of over 50 million has had as high a number of political assassinations or attempted assassinations.[8] These facts raise many serious issues about American society. Why has the United States, with its commitment to justice, been so susceptible to this type of crime and do those that perpetrate these crimes alter the course of history?

In a very real sense, the crimes that have been committed in history, especially American history, have not altered the course of human events in the manner the offense had intended to generate. The assassination of Martin Lither King Jr. which had been hoped to derail the civil rights movement did no such thing, in a strong reality it only added to the overwhelming need to further the stride of the movement towards equality. The assassination of Robert Kennedy did not alter the United States relationship with Israel. In fact, when Nixon became president the relationship between the United States and Israel was fermented even stronger, the total opposite of what Sirhan Sirhan had hoped. More often than not, even when a crime is committed in hopes of banding citizens together against the government, the assassin will always be seen as the villain and their goal of anarchy foiled. John Wilkes Booth had hoped that by killing Abraham Lincoln, the Confederate States of America would again regain their strength and continue to fight and eventually win the American Civil War.[9] He was wrong and in the days after Lincoln's death, Booth realized the error of his judgment and knew history would vilify him with its judgment. Of course more examples can be cited and more instances discussed, but in the end the death did occur and the first piece of any of these assassins goals is absolutely recognized.

The hope and drive that these leaders brought to the threshold was stopped, their fire put out, and their essence fades. Robert Kennedy knew this when he spoke in Cleveland. He knew that the goal of an assassin was never truly achieved, because the act of assassination has always meant to be the part of something bigger and that goal dies with the first stroke of action. Kennedy continued,

> *No wrongs have ever been righted by riots and civil disorders. A sniper is only a coward, not a hero; and an uncontrolled, uncontrollable mob is only the voice of madness, not the voice of reason.*

In the wake of the assassination of Martin Luther King, Robert Kennedy demanded that the American people not use the same type of violence against each other that was used against him. He cites "reason" and the need of the people to use it in order to preserve peace rather than riot. The definition of reason is a statement offered in explanation or justification, a rational ground or motive, a sufficient ground of explanation or of logical defense, something that supports a conclusion or explains a fact.[10] Kennedy called on the better judgment of the people to use reason and not lower themselves to the voice of trepidation.

Robert Kennedy knew, as well as anyone, the anger being felt and hatred building up against those that had committed this crime. The need for action must be allowed to be used properly. Blacks must not target whites out of hatred. He was using these words in the hopes that mob action would not be used, pleading that by using such methods unbecoming of the voice of reason was to lower their humanity to the level of those who perpetrated the crime. Too often in history reason has been pushed aside and in its place the quick need to find answers is discovered through missteps and wrong decisions. Many times, one can only look at history and be burdened by the sadness to which it reiterates. History is the search to understand and the need to discover who people are as a society. Many, when researching and exploring the past ask themselves the question: what, as a society, have we accomplished throughout history? People do not ask themselves this question with the hope of discovering wrongdoing. Instead people move forward hoping to find that as a society, people were the best they could be. As a society and those that examine American history have found, the American past has been one of triumph and tragedy, hope and despair, and glory and chaos.

Although American history has had its share of "black marks" throughout its existence with its policies towards African Americans, Native Americans, immigrants, and women, it has been the lack of empathy towards one another that has become most troubling in American history. More recently, in the twenty-first century, Americans arguably have started to care less about one another than ever before. There are many people that care less and less about their fellow human beings, and have become indifferent towards one another. Looking back on history, understanding how important reason is, all too often reason is easily excluded from the rationale of those being studied.

In a society that instead of funding children's health care, that would lead to the coverage of millions of American children currently not insured, the American government in its place wastes money on a war without end. It has been said that the future lay in what our children can provide to society, but society remains seemingly ignorant on the need to protect that very commodity. Society and politicians today will again decry the need of universal healthcare, because it resembles socialism. Yet at the same time, government sponsored universal programs are all ready in full swing. Would Americans ask for the privatization of the police force, or fire protection agencies, or the library, or even the post office? By allowing these organizations to resemble the socialist policies that people are supposed to fear, is that not a double standard? Therefore, I ask if one can have universal programs in some parts of American life, why not health care? Why not education?

First of all, let it be said, socialism is not the answer for America. In reality, the proposal is for young and old Americans to not have to worry that one day they will lose their entire life savings because they cannot afford their medical bills. Can society seriously stand by and allow eighteen thousand Americans to die every single year, just because they lack the ability to afford health care?[11] Imagine a society where Americans did not have to worry about health insurance, did not have to worry about college loans, instead they were free to live and grow. This is not the sponsorship of socialism or communism, or any other "ism," rather the pledge that all Americans begin to help one another on a greater level. Critics might object and say in doing so taxes in America would skyrocket and why should some individuals pay higher taxes in order to help other Americans. This concern, should in great reality remedy itself. Taxes in America are all ready high but with this new avenue, those Americans that live in fear of being injured and are not able to pay their bills would be insured and taken care of. If higher taxes mean that everyone has health insurance it is believed many people would subscribe.

On April 26, 1968, Robert Kennedy was asked by a student at the Indiana University Medical School how he intended to pay for federal programs geared at social issues. He answered,

> From you. Let me say something about the tenor of that question and some of the other questions. There are people in this country who suffer. I look around this room and I don't see many black faces who are going to be doctors. You can

talk about where the money will come from . . . Part of civilized society is to let people go to medical school who come from the ghettos. You don't see many people coming out of the ghettos or off the Indian reservations to medical school. You are the privileged ones here. It's easy to sit back and say it's the fault of the federal government, but it's our responsibility, too. It's our society, not just our government, that spends twice as much on pets as on the poverty program. It's the poor who carry the major burden of the struggle in Vietnam. You sit here as white medical students while black people carry the burden of the fighting in Vietnam.[12]

The problems of society affect everyone, not just those that need the help of the federal government or the help from social programs geared at their survival. Therefore, the understanding is that Americans are all in this together. When one section of our society experiences turmoil the entire portion suffers. Everyone has an obligation to assist those that cannot afford to help themselves.

I am tired of hearing this labeled a "leftist liberal agenda." I consider myself a liberal, but I more importantly consider myself an American citizen and dislike seeing other people living in America, native or immigrant, suffer. Whether labeled as a conservative republican or liberal democrat, the description means nothing. Human beings have a role to play in society. How is it that some people live in beautiful homes, while others live in squalor? If a tax increase means that some of my money has saved a young boy or girl from having to worry about getting sick, because they have no ability to afford health insurance, then as a human being, I would gladly have taxes increased.

There has been an outpouring of support from influential politicians and humanitarians like Al Gore, businessmen like Sir Richard Branson, and many world leaders pushing for more programs geared at helping Americans in need as well as countless programs geared at solving the climate crisis in the world. Society has looked to our past and moved forward with the belief that at one point Americans had done something wrong and now must use reason to fix the major issues that affect American society today. This growth of support is an indication of the level to which society can and will grow. Yet there are still other serious problems in America. That distress on our American journey has become the great level of violence which still exists and continues unabated. Robert Kennedy stated,

Whenever any American's life is taken by another American unnecessarily— whether it is done in the name of the law or in the defiance of the law, by one man or a gang, in cold blood or in passion, in an attack of violence or in response to violence—whenever we tear at the fabric of the life which another man has painfully and clumsily woven for himself and his children, the whole nation is degraded.

It is suggested that everyone reading this book, take the time to pick up a newspaper or go on the internet and read the headlines of some of the most important news of that given day and see what it is comprised of. Most of it will be the happenings of celebrities, sports scores, the calculated mistakes by the current administration, and also a level of violence in the news that is truly unsettling. Not too long ago, there was an article about three West Palm Beach teenagers that assaulted and gang raped a mother and her twelve year old son. The three teens broke into the house of the mother and child. They sexual assaulted the mother, beat the child, and at gun point forced the mother to rape her own son.[13] One can only become absolutely sick to their stomach when reading a description of what took place. Yet, unfortunately this type of crime is only the tip of the iceberg of what someone would find in a month or even a weeks worth of news.

In Acworth, Georgia, three boys ages eight and nine were held on charges of kidnapping and raping an eleven year old girl in the woods near a suburban apartment complex. The victim stated that an "eight year old boy and two nine year old boys that she had been playing with earlier pulled her into a wooded area, where one of the boys raped her."[14] This again is another incident of cruelty and an indication that the level of violence is continuing and the perpetrators are getting younger. Now, this book will not attempt to conclude why violence has risen or even why these crimes are committed or why the person that committed them did it. Instead, this work shows how the level of violence has risen and instead of finding out why it took place, try and find a better path to help stop these instances from occurring through the words of a man that lived in one of the most violent years in American history.

Now these two incidents of rape and apathy are two articles among countless others describing disturbing scenes of violence that shake every state in the country. Just recently the Federal Bureau of Investigation released a report stating that hate crimes in the United States rose by six percent in 2006. The report stated that,

> Police across the nation reported 7,722 criminal incidents in 2006 targeting victims or property as a result of bias against a particular race, religion, sexual orientation, ethnic or national origin or physical or mental disability. That was up 7.8 percent from the 7,163 incidents reported in 2005.[15]

The point is that innocent people are victimized each and every day. American lives are taken so unnecessarily. Whether it is rape, a hate crime or murder, the victims of crime are normal Americans with normal ambitions and dreams for the future. For someone to come into the mixture of that ambition and stir it up, adding their devious assertion is in all regards, an act of horror. As Americans and citizens of morality, people have the right to live and pursue life without fear that they are going to be victimized and have their lives taken away from them by the criminal actions of others. This can be perceived as the greatest demonstration of violence, the taking away of ones right to live and experience the possibility that they have to offer society. It is sad that an individual can leave and go to work in the morning, kissing their wife or husband goodbye, and in the process of the day fall victim to senseless violence leaving their significant other alone. Violence instills fear in people and that fear makes people live their lives differently. Whether it is the act of locking a door at night, or looking over one's shoulder when walking to a car, or even carrying mace in a pocket or purse, fear is the success of violence. If fear continues to control our lives, it means that society has allowed the endless violence to be the victor.

As Kennedy tried to point out in this section of his speech, whether a person was killed in a random mugging, because of a love triangle, as vigilante justice, or during rioting over the disagreements between the people and the state, in the end the nation as a whole can be scarred and degraded. If society answers aggressive action with the same level of hostility it becomes not only a combination of failure, but also a lethal mixture of injustice. During the 1968 Democratic Convention protesting outside was met with violence from the local authority. When a man has his back against the door and violence is used by the same authority being protested against, many will use the same level of violence to fight back. Within that mixture there are deadly consequences.

In today's society, there has been a twenty five percent increase in the number of cases in which police, prison guards, and other law enforcement authorities have used excessive force or other tactics to violate victim's civil rights from 2001 to 2007. This type of action will not help to diminish the use of violence but heighten it out of fear that those that are supposed to protect will use violence as well.[16] It should be understood that if an individual is put up against a wall, they will fight back. As the late Gerard Vanderhaar, writer and Professor Emeritus of Religion and Peace Studies at Christian Brothers University in Memphis, Tennessee, once stated,

> We challenge the culture of violence when we ourselves act in the certainty that violence is no longer acceptable, that it's tired and outdated no matter how many cling to it in the stubborn belief that it still works and that it's still valid.[17]

Violence must be looked at as unacceptable and not be used in retaliation for hostility used against those trying to move away from the wall. When violence is used against anyone, many will then retaliate with more violence, even more severe than was used against them. Therefore, those that must not use force are those with the instruction to serve and protect.

On May 7, 2008 it was reported that at least a dozen officers were videotaped pulling three suspects out of an automobile throwing them to the ground and beating them. In the video at least eight officers were seen kicking, punching, or striking suspects with batons while the men lie restrained on the ground.[18] Two of the suspects were struck at least twenty times each.[19] It was stated that the officer's emotions got the best of them. They were emotional because the previous Saturday, Sgt. Stephen Liczbinski was shot and killed with an assault rifle while attempting to apprehend bank robbery suspects.[20]

While the death of the sergeant was tragic, it did not give the officers permission to use such excessive force. If they use a violent procedure in the criminal justice arena, then they will be met in kind with that same aggression. They need to use less force and less brutality and therefore not give others a reason to use brutal techniques against them. If the police act according to immoral standards, so will those they are there to protect. It is a disgrace that in the first ten months of 2007 there were forty two law enforcement prosecutions, a sixty six percent increase than from all of 2002 and sixty one percent increase from 1997.[21] It is best to lead by example and if this is the example that law enforcement agencies want to set, then our work to curb the level of violence will be more difficult as the road gets wider.

Robert Kennedy had witnessed how the level of violence could rise and become unmanageable. His words of wisdom and disdain for using riots as violent tools of change were pure. They cannot be used as tools of change, for a weapon of the same caliber will surely result with the same effect. This was of course in the wake of the assassination of Martin Luther King Jr. so Kennedy arguably knew full well that black Americans would riot in the streets, angry at the death of their moral leader. Kennedy sought to suggest that the course of action they were willing to angrily use, was the same level of violence that had taken away their leader in the first place. He asked for everyone to take a step back and reflect. He asked for citizens to consider a non-violent approach, an approach championed by the slain King.

Robert Kennedy at that time was a presidential nominee candidate and did not want the country's image to be tarnished by the violence taking place on the streets of the major cities in the country. Still today, society has looked towards Robert Kennedy's words for comfort and understanding. Americans too often watch the news and see murder cases dealing with crimes of passion such as the O.J. Simpson case and Scott Peterson case, and too often are witness to a growing level of gang violence that makes cities in America unsafe for average Americans. Robert Kennedy at the end of this section of his speech was trying to tell his listeners that whenever violence is used as a tool of aggression and whenever an individual becomes a victim, the nation as a whole becomes flawed. The same person that becomes a victim is a person that has woven their own story, their own history, and with their passing the fabric which they have created their lives with is torn. Lost is the life they created for their families. Kennedy used the fabric analogy eloquently and its meaning was powerful.

What people must come to realize is that in today's society any individual can become a victim of violence, and are just as likely to become a victim as anyone else. Look into the eyes of a stranger or loved one and think about how shattered the lives of all around them would be if violence claimed them as its next victim. This is not the death of old age, or car crash, or even an illness, it is rather the death taken at the hands of one that could have stopped. The knowledge that a person is dead because one person acquiesced to his violent thoughts is a difficult pill to swallow. It is at this point that people should realize that the level of violence is intolerable and unnecessary. There is no reason that any individual should not come home, because of the actions of another. Robert Kennedy drove this point home at this time in his speech.

The last section of Robert Kennedy's speech in this chapter is the following,

> *'Among free men,'* said Abraham Lincoln, *'there can be no successful appeal from the ballot to the bullet; and those who take such appeal are sure to lost their cause and pay the costs.'*

There was no better person that Robert Kennedy could have quoted in his speech than the "Great Emancipator" Abraham Lincoln. In a time when there was a need to stop violence and curb racial tensions, the quoting of Lincoln provides guidance to a nation in need of another hero. The loss of President John F. Kennedy, Martin Luther King Jr., and countless others in Vietnam, as well as on the streets of American cities, had deviated and distracted America from its path to helping people. Robert Kennedy's use of Lincoln was crucial to the success of this speech and its placement in the speech was incredible. He draws on Lincoln's image and words to guide a nation still divided over racial issues. Lincoln had attempted to give black Americans rights in the closing of the Civil War, but his assassination possibly prolonged racial injustices in America that had been resolved four years before the "Mindless Menace of Violence" speech, with the Civil Rights Act of 1964. Even with this major piece of legislation combined with the Voting Rights Act of 1965, the country was still bitterly divided over racial issues. With the deaths of John F. Kennedy and Martin Luther King Jr., many Americans, especially blacks, were overcome with fear that the same emotions that developed when Abraham Lincoln was assassinated, would again be conjured up. This fear was that their role in society would be jeopardized. Robert Kennedy references Lincoln so that he may speak to America almost on behalf of Lincoln to reorient America to the path which Lincoln envisioned. Kennedy does this to assure all, of his same commitment to human justice and human rights.

The quote that Kennedy used was from a letter that Lincoln had written. Lincoln was invited to attend a function in Springfield, Illinois, the objective of which was to discuss the maintenance of the Union. Unfortunately because of the important duties he had to attend to in Washington D.C., he could not leave the capital, so instead he wrote a letter to James C. Conkling. Lincoln's letter was also in response to a letter he had received from Conkling protesting the Emaciation Proclamation, as well as the creation of all black regiments to fight in the Civil War for the Union. Although Conkling professed his deepest loyalty to the Union, Lincoln answered his letter regarding black regiments by saying, "You say you will not fight to free Negroes. Some of them seem willing to fight for you." Lincoln went on,

> The Father of Waters again goes unvexed to the sea. Thanks to the great Northwest for it; nor yet wholly to them. . . . The sunny South, too, in more colors than one, also lent a helping hand. On the spot, their part of the history was jotted down in black and white. The job was a great national one, and let none be slighted who bore an honorable part in it. And while those who have cleared the great river may well be proud, even that is not all. It is hard to say that anything has been more bravely and well done than at Antietam, Murfreesboro, Gettysburg, and on many fields of less note. Nor must Uncle Sam's web-feet be forgotten . . . Thanks to all. For the great republic–for the principle it lives by and keeps alive–for man's vast future–thanks to all.[22]

Lincoln was conveying to the recipient of the letter the importance of the fight they were engaged in. From Gettysburg to the Battle of the Ironclads, every battle had significance in the great endeavor to restore the Union.

> Peace does not appear so distant as it did. I hope it will come soon and come to stay; and so come as to be worth the keeping in all future time. It will then have been proved that *among freemen there can be no successful appeal from the ballot to the bullet, and that they who take such appeal are sure to lose their case and pay the cost.* And there will be some black men who can remember that with silent tongue and clenched teeth and steady eye and well-poised bayonet they have helped mankind on to this great consummation; while I fear there will be some white ones unable to forget that with malignant heart and deceitful speech they have striven to hinder it.[23]

It was a poetic and eye opening letter written by Lincoln. He professed his need to save the country and to do so would require the assistance of African

Americans. Although many whites were not willing to fight for them, Lincoln knew that blacks were willing to fight for all. After all, blacks during the Civil War had the most to lose and the most to gain by a Union victory. A Union success insured their freedom. As Lincoln reiterates in the beginning of the passage in the letter, he feels that an end to the bloody conflict was finally in sight. An end to the conflict, as Lincoln believed, would prove that violence and separation can never succeed in a free and just society.

In the first section of the "Mindless Menace of Violence" speech it has gone from detailing how politics takes a back seat to the need to discuss moral matters and ended with a quote given by Abraham Lincoln. Lincoln discussed how secession and rebellion as well as violence in the wake of political issues can never successfully accomplish the ultimate goal. One can never go from elections to rebellion in a peaceful manner, violence will always ensue, and the final result will be to the detriment of all. In that regard, it was assured that the rebel through failure will pay the cost of his future. The same can be said of those that commit acts of violence against the innocent. In the first part of Kennedy's speech, he tried to convince his listeners to end the senseless violence in America, to stop attacking white Americans and stop attacking black Americans. By ending with Abraham Lincoln's quote, Kennedy signaled the need to remember that at one point in our history there was a great disagreement on racial issues. The result of this nation's miscalculated avoidance of the issue of race in American society led to the deaths of 620,000 Americans.

Kennedy tried to set the stage for hope by saying that, yes King had died, but violence could never bring about his resurrection. There could be no act of kindness or violence that could change what history had already sealed. The need was to move forward and remember the message that King had lived to defend. Instead of degrading his memory in violence and draping his coffin in blood, fulfill his vision with peace. Robert Kennedy appealed to the better nature of men, not the human instinct of men. He attempted to look past what history had told him, and instead brought comfort through hope and wisdom. Patrick Henry once spoke out in defense of liberty and justice and vilified all of those that sought to destroy the bonds of republican government that had begun to take shape in America preceding the American Revolution. Society must look to his words for inspiration as they combat the institutions of violence and the evils of indifference. He stated,

> It is in vain, sir, to extenuate the matter. Gentlemen may cry, "Peace! Peace!"— But there is no peace. The war is actually begun! The next gale that sweeps from the north will bring to our ears the clash of resounding arms! Our brethren are already in the field! Why stand we here idle? What is it that gentlemen wish? What would they have? Is life so dear, or peace so sweet, as to be purchased at

the price of chains and slavery? Forbid it, Almighty God! I know not what course others may take; but as for me, give me liberty or give me deth![24]

NOTES

1. Jeff Flock, "5 Dead, 11 Wounded in Arkansas School Shooting," *CNN.com*, 24 March 1998, <www.cnn.com/US/9803/24/school.shooting.folo/> (9 April 2008).

2. David Kocieniewski and Gary Gately, "Man shoots 11, killing 4 Girls, in Amish School," *International Herald Tribune.com*, 3 October 2006, <www.iht.com/articles/ 2006/10/03/america/web.1003slay.php> (28 March 2008).

3. Rebecca Cathcart, "Boy's Killing, Labeled a Hate Crime, Stuns Town," *New York Times.com*, 23 February 2008, <www.nytimes.com/2008/02/23/us/23oxnard.html> (22 March 2008).

4. Russell Goldman, and Richard Esposito, "Illinois Shooter Planned Campus Shooting for at Least a Week," *ABC News.com*, 15 February 2008, <www.abcnews.go.com/US/ story?id=429308> (24 March 2008).

5. Robert V. Remini, *The Life of Andrew Jackson* (New York: Perennial Classics, 1988), 296-298.

6. Remini, 297-298.

7. James Mckinley, *Assassinations in America* (New York: Harper and Row, 1977), 100.

8. Mckinley, 100.

9. James M. McPherson, *Battle Cry of Freedom: The Civil War Era* (New York: Ballantine Books, 1988), 893.

10. *Merriam and Webster Dictionary and Thesaurus Online*, 2008, <http://www.merriam-webster.com/> (4 April 2008).

11. United Nations Development Report, "The Impact of Health Insurance Coverage on Health Disparities in the United States," Human Development Report, UNDP, 2005.

12. Robert F. Kennedy, "From You," (Speech delivered at the Indiana University Medical School on 26 April 1968). Robert F. Kennedy Senate Files Archive in the John F. Kennedy Library, part of the National Archives.

13. Associated Press, "3 Teens Indicted in Rape of Mother, Son," *MSNBC.com*, 19 July 2007, <www.msnbc.msn.com/id/19852756/> (2 September 2007).

14. Associated Press, "Boys Ages 8 and 9 Charged with Rape," *FoxNews.com*, 19 November 2007, <www.foxnews.com/story/0,2933,312146,00.html> (2 February 2008).

15. Michael J. Sniffen, "Hate Crimes Rose 8 Percent in 2006," *Washingtonpost.com*, 19 November 2007, <www.washingtonpost.com/wp-dyn/content/ article/2007/11/19/ AR2007111900607.html> (8 February 2008).

16. Kevin Johnson, "Police Brutality Cases on Rise since 9/11," *USA Today.com*, 18 December 2007, <www.usatoday.com/news/nation/2007-12-17-Copmisconduct_N.html> (23 January 2008).

17. Gerard Vanderhaar, *Quotes*, 2008, <http://www.gvanderhaar.org/> (13 February 2008).

18. Mythili Rao, "Mayor: Officers in Taped Beating will be Fired," *CNN.com*, 19 May 2008, <www.cnn.com/2008/CRIME/05/19/police.beating/index.html> (19 May 2008).

19. Mythili Rao, "Mayor: Officers in Taped Beating will be Fired," *CNN.com*, 19 May 2008, <www.cnn.com/2008/CRIME/05/19/police.beating/index.html> (19 May 2008).

20. Associated Press, "Suspect Charged in Philadelphia Cop Killing," *CNN.com*, 4 May 2008, <www.cnn.com/2008/CRIME/05/04/officer.shot. philadelphia.ap/index.html> (18 May 2008).

21. Kevin Johnson, "Police Brutality Cases on Rise since 9/11," *USA Today*, 18 December 2007.

22. Letter from Abraham Lincoln to James C. Conkling, 26 August 1863.

23. Letter from Abraham Lincoln to James C. Conkling, 26 August 1863.

24. Patrick Henry, "Give Me Liberty, or Give Me Death," (Speech delivered at the St. Johns Church in Richmond, Virginia on 23 March 1775), Patrick Henry Committee, St. John's Church.

Chapter Three

Sickness of Our Soul

Few will have the greatness to bend history; but each of us can work to change a small portion of events . . . Each time a man stands up for an ideal, or acts to improve the lot of others, or strikes out against injustice, he sends forth a tiny ripple of hope, and crossing each other from a million different centers of energy and daring, those ripples build a current which can sweep down the mightiest walls of oppression and resistance.

—Robert F. Kennedy

While I write this work, I am twenty-five years old and perceive a future that can be whatever I make of it. I see wonderful things that this country, as a moral beacon, can do and advancements it can support. I use the message of Robert Kennedy to remind everyone of a time when individuals inspired change and embodied greatness. That type of leadership seems to have faded, but it can still be achieved. On March 16, 1968 Robert Kennedy announced his candidacy for the presidency of the United States of America. He stood in the caucus room of the Old State Office building, the same room that his brother had used to declare his candidacy in 1960.[1] He began with the same sentence and declared that he ran to "close the gaps that now exist between black and white, between rich and poor, between young and old" and stated that the times he lived in were not "ordinary times and this was not an ordinary election. At stake is not simply the leadership of our party and even our country. It is our right to the moral leadership of this planet."[2]

Today, in 2008, America still suffers from this need to secure our right as a country to be that moral leadership in the world. People look for leadership to show they are worthy of that responsibility, but as of late have been represented by a governing power that lacks the moral leadership that Kennedy

45

embodied. After the death of his brother he changed. As Thurston Clark stated,

> A deep, black grief gripped Robert Kennedy in the months following his brother's assassination. He lost weight, fell into melancholy silences, wore his brother's clothes, smoked the cigars his brother had liked, and imitated his mannerisms. Eventually his grief went underground, but it sometimes erupted in geysers of tears.[3]

Kennedy was more involved, more compassionate and greatly wanted to affect the outcome of history. Through his leadership a message of hope and determination was broadcast for an entire nation that was being inflicted with moral wounds. In 1968, the nation was wounded by the war in Vietnam and three summers of inner-city riots. Whether it was footage on television of American troops committing atrocities against an enemy they believed capable of such evil or witnessed police and federal troops patrolling the streets of American cities, Americans were uncertain of their future. They looked to Robert Kennedy for guidance and inspiration. He denounced the war in Vietnam and spoke of hope for the future. In 1968 he inspired a nation and in 2008 he inspired this author.

Our country faces the same challenges now that it faced then, however the places have different names and the people different faces, but the ideas and issues are the same. America is involved in a doomed and unnecessary war and lives in a severely divided state. It needs now, more then ever, the moral leadership Kennedy inspired a nation to believe in. I feel inspired by his words and want to live my life according to the moral leadership he outlined and to which this nation must follow if it is to live up to its creed and obligations to all living things. Like many Americans, I live today with the world at my finger tips and all I have to do is make the leap.

At my Providence College graduation I had the pleasure of having John O'Hurley, class of '76 at Providence College, give the commencement address. Most of America and the world know John O'Hurley as the business tycoon J. Peterman of the J. Peterman Company on the NBC hit sitcom *Seinfeld*. As a huge fan of the show, it was exciting to have Mr. O'Hurley provide the commencement address. But, on May 21, 2006, it was not his comedy that struck a cord, rather his candor and words of wisdom for the future of our generation. During his address he told all of us to live what he called an "Extraordinary Life" and provided what he laughingly phrased as *"The Peterman Guide to the Extraordinary Life."* He told us,

> An extraordinary life, as I've come to understand it, has three simple elements. And these elements are common to everyone who has ever taken that journey.

An extraordinary life is a life of achievement, a life of meaning, and a life of re-flection. Achievement begins with imagination . . . What you imagine has value. It is tragic as it is true, but the greatest plans on earth still lie in the minds of peo-ple who still think that everybody else has a better idea than they do. Dream large, dream small, but trust what you imagine, because what you day-dream about is what you are supposed to do . . . When you trust what you imagine, amazing things happen. You become willing to make the leap to achieve what you imagine. I say 'leap' because nothing worth anything is ever close at hand. It's always farther away than a comfortable reach. It involves risk. But, believe me, if you leap, the net will appear. When you leap, the net will appear.[4]

John O'Hurley reminded me of something very important that day. It was that life is not easy and anything that is worth something will involve risk. As Mr. O'Hurley stipulated, in order for life to be extraordinary it must have a sem-blance of simple elements. These elements are achievement, meaning, and re-flection. If one has these important elements, their life can be classified as ex-traordinary. Another major point that Mr. O'Hurley stated in his address was the fact that the dreamers are the ones that imagine what they are supposed to do with their lives. I remember another quote by Sir Thomas E. Lawrence. He said,

All men dream, but not equally. Those who dream by night in the dusty recesses of their minds, wake in the day to find that it was vanity: but the dreamers of the day are dangerous men, for they may act on their dreams with open eyes, to make them possible.[5]

Individuals that dream with their eyes open are the people to admire, people that are filled and bursting with passion unlike many other instrumental peo-ple in society and in history. In all reality, Robert F. Kennedy dreamed with his eyes wide open. He had a vision of how society should be and he hoped would become. The type of person John O'Hurley was talking about was the type of person that is filled with all the qualities that can change the world. Robert Kennedy had these qualities and had the ability to inspire a nation to take the leap with him. America today searches for another individual who, as a nation, they can take that same leap with.

John O'Hurley discussed further his idea of an extraordinary life and how it can be achieved and viewed in the world today. He said the following words,

But achievement alone does not an extraordinary life make. Achievement alone is not enough. Hollywood and the rest of the entertainment world are filled with peo-ple who seem to accomplish much, but live lives that are otherwise without much value, except for their ability to fill the pages of magazines that seem to dedicate themselves weekly to their confusion. An extraordinary life has meaning, and meaning comes only from love. Love for another . . . and love for yourself. When we learn to love another, we experience the joy of selflessness because we extend ourselves for their good. When we love ourselves, and perhaps this is the toughest kind of love, we learn that we are a gift. We protect that gift and avoid destructive behavior. We develop a sense of humor about ourselves and the world around us. As G.K. Chesterton so poignantly wrote, 'Angels fly because they take themselves lightly.'[6]

I think John O'Hurley was correct with his description of what it takes to have a life that becomes extraordinary. In society today when the level of violence seems to constantly rise, his words are very important and moving. He was telling an entire auditorium of students ready to take on the world that they could make a difference. He told everyone there that they can move mountains if they are willing to make a leap. He was not saying that it was hard in the real world and most of our attempts would end in failure. Rather, he told us that one can be assured that they will fail if they do not try. For the first time in this author's life he heard a speech, first hand, which changed his life. John O'Hurley provided words of wisdom and thoughts of encouragement. He told the students that they could leave that arena and strive to make the world a better place. In the end, Mr. O'Hurley stated,

> The final aspect of the extraordinary life is what makes it all worthwhile, and that is perspective. You have heard people tell you, 'Never look back, always look forward.' I say nonsense—always look back and as often as you can. It is the only way you know how far you have come . . . That half-look over your shoulder at the child you were and the person you've become, and all that you have achieved in between, and all that you have achieved is your story, your history. The enjoyment of that progress will make you appreciate all those who were part of your story . . . And from your appreciation will come what is perhaps the greatest virtue of the extraordinary life—and that is generosity. You will give back, because you know you have been given so much.[7]

There is not one person in this country that does not posses the power to make this world a better place. When will our society realize that everyone will be able to live an extraordinary life? Each and every person in the country and world can make a significant difference that can help change the course of life on this planet. Each American has the ability to use the tools which they have gained during their journey to help those that have no ability to help themselves. As John O'Hurley stated, generosity is crucial to living an extraordinary life. There is something to be said of the power and impact that the spoken word can have on those that open their ears to listen. Some may have slept, others listened to music, but I acknowledged and respected the message that John O'Hurley provided that afternoon in 2006.

In the final analysis it is with happiness that Mr. O'Hurley did not use the term, "human nature," when referring to the capabilities of human beings. While John O'Hurley's speech inspires people to live a productive and amazing life, it is important to use that understanding to appreciate the message that Robert Kennedy provides in the second quarter of the "Mindless Menace of Violence" speech. There was, in one instance, a major similarity between a portion of John O'Hurley's address in regards to achievement and Robert Kennedy's speech in this section.

Robert Kennedy started this section of his speech by illuminating the fact that Americans today ignore the horror surrounding them. Robert Kennedy stated,

Yet we seemingly tolerate a rising level of violence that ignores our common humanity and our claims to civilization alike.

As has been discussed, violence in society has continued to grow at a rate that should shock the average American. Although appalling, sadly it is not surprising. A couple of weeks ago I went online and looked at the news and to my horror read an article from Pittsburgh. The crime involved a ten month old baby that had died after "being raped and beaten by her mother's boyfriend while the mother was at work. The infant would end up dying at Pittsburgh's Children Hospital, two days after the assault."[8] The Allegheny County medical examiner's office ruled her death a homicide, saying she died from "multi-system organ failure precipitated by her injuries from the assault."[9] Not long after reading about this incident, I read about a Philadelphia mother that,

Bought guns and bomb-making material to indulge her socially outcast 14-year-old son. She was being accused of buying her son, who planned a Columbine-like attack on a school . . . a 9mm semiautomatic rifle and black powder used to make grenades.[10]

These types of crimes ignore the common decency that humanity strives to protect. A mother buying her child weapons after all the school shootings that America has gone through in the last ten years seems ignorant of universal understanding. Americans live in a society were it is common, almost normal, to fear the possibility of school shootings and yet people still provide their children with access to all types of weaponry.

Although the Second Amendment allows for Americans to have the right to own weapons, there are many weapons that have no right being allowed into the hands of Americans. While the right to "keep and bear arms" has been the issue of debate for decades, the right to own certain types of guns, especially assault weapons, should be banned on legal and ethical grounds. The fact that in 2004 the assault weapon ban on the The Brady Handgun

Violence Prevention Act or "Brady Bill" expired without a fundamental protest from those that object was careless and outrageous.[11] After all, 2004 was an election year, which allowed for many issues to be overlooked while deciding who to vote for. In a year when the war in Iraq was being perceived as a success, why would anyone challenge the National Rifle Association and their republican allies on such an important need to renew the ban? This is where the moral leadership in the United States failed, and has continued to do so. While many did attempt to challenge the expiration of such a necessity, their support lacked the will of the citizenry and in its wake the rules of reason became victim to the rules of complacency.

While the ban expired and there are reports of parents buying weapons for their own children, people perceive what appears to be a serious lack of empathy on the part of countless citizens in this country. These types of acts and these types of actions go against everything this nation stands for in regards to its obligation to protect its citizens. The fact that Americans are allowed to own semi-automatic weapons is a clear example of how the message that Robert Kennedy provided is still ignored and the level of violence allowed to strengthen further. Americans will not make changes on the war to end poverty if they do nothing to provide a stable economic structure in the United States. America will not make changes in the war on violence if it allows the people that perpetrate violence the means to own weapons that inflict brutality.

While I oppose the Second Amendment as it is interpreted, it should be seen as an outrage by all and a calamity that individuals in this country can own certain weapons, which have no hunting or reasonable purpose or capability. As James Brady, who the "Brady Bill" is named after, once commented regarding gun control, "For target shooting, that's okay. Get a license and go to the range. For defense of the home, that's why we have police departments." James Scott Brady was the Assistant to the President and White House Press Secretary under President Ronald Reagan. After becoming permanently disabled, nearly being killed, as a result of an assassination attempt on Reagan in 1981, Brady became a strong supporter of gun control in America.

On December 5, 2007 a gunman opened fire in a Nebraska mall killing nine innocent people that had done nothing more than go shopping for holiday gifts. A news report stated,

> Witnesses said the gunman fired down on shoppers from a third-floor balcony of the Von Maur store using what police said was an SKS assault rifle they found at the scene. The shooter, identified by police as 19 year old Robert A. Hawkins, was found dead on the third floor with a self-inflicted gunshot wound. Omaha Police Chief Thomas Warren said the shooting appeared to be random. He would not release the victim's identities and gave no motive for the attack.[12]

The shooter described as a "troubled young man who was like a lost pound puppy that nobody wanted," took innocent people's lives before killing himself. It is this complete and total lack of caring about each other that Robert Kennedy warned could and would happen if nothing was done to curb the level of violence in the United States. The sad fact regarding this incident was that it was not the first but the second mall shooting in 2007. In February, "nine people were shot, five of them fatally, at Trolley Square Mall in Salt Lake City. The gunman, 18 year old Sulejman Talovic, was shot and killed by police."[13] In the case of the nineteen year old Nebraska mall shooter, he left a suicide note saying that this shooting would make him famous. Thus, it was a premeditated killing, meaning that he thought about carrying the act out and followed through with it, but the targets were random people. What more of an example does one need to show the terrible cost that violence inflicts on American civilians every single day? The trouble is that people are becoming used to this type of violence and the fact that this shooter, like the Columbine shooting in 1999, was a young adult is a further indicator that the level of violence is raising to seemingly unprecedented levels.

Yet, many in America refuse to realize or rather refuse to accept that there is something wrong. Many refuse to look at the evidence in front of them and demand change. Most would rather focus on insulting political leaders, or others find reasons to declare liberals evil or conservatives incorrect. It is sad that America has become a place where political opinion will make someone vilified instead of listened to. If someone, whether a politician or average citizen, has an opinion that is unique or against the common understanding, they will be tongue-lashed. Instead of debating those ideas and looking for common ground to stand on and agreeing on a common goal for change, there are many, especially in the media, that force the average American to remain distant and out of touch with reality. Society seems to dislike those that ask questions, and those that do are attacked from both the right and the left. Hate continues to be used by many in the media to create an atmosphere of fear. Through fear they take away people's ability to be proud of their political opinion. Those that demand society agree with their political opinions use the wrath of their hate and spew political venom that creates doubt in people's minds when it comes to issues that matter most. If society allows those types of people to successfully cloud the major issues of today with the mist of hate, then it is possible that they too will push society away from the true point of the American political arena. Yet, even when they use their terrible rhetoric, in the end it serves to only fasten those of the moral high ground to their issues and work harder to show that America is not a place of hatred or insults, but rather a place that works to improve the quality of life for all its citizens.

In the end, society looks for new avenues and new paths to create change. Robert Kennedy discussed,

We calmly accept newspaper reports of civilian slaughter in far-off lands.

Robert Kennedy was living in the midst of America's war in Vietnam. On January 27, 1968, General Westmoreland told the nation that the enemy has "experienced failure," and he expressed optimism for success in 1968.[14] Of course as history has written, it would only be three days later on Tet, the Buddhist lunar New Year, that enemy troops launched their most massive offensive of the war. These major strikes against most cities and villages controlled by the South Vietnamese were incredible. They showed that not only were the Vietcong and North Vietnam not beaten, but the war was going to last much longer than Washington perhaps had anticipated. As author and historian Terry Anderson described,

> Tet was the first event of 1968 that demonstrated the sixties had become the 'Decade of Tumult and Change.' This one year was as significant as any during the twentieth century, for it radically altered social, cultural, and political realities, and that was demonstrated as 1968 exploded 'over race, youth, violence, lifestyles, and, above all, over the Vietnam War.'[15]

Kennedy spoke of the slaughter being perpetrated in Vietnam and the senseless bloodshed being spilled in the name of democracy. Robert Kennedy was one of the first and most outspoken senators against the war in Vietnam, becoming intertwined with the anti-war movement taking shape in the country. Kennedy spoke in 1968 at Kansas State University and he told students there that the country was "deep in a malaise of the spirit" and suffering from "a deep crisis of confidence."[16] The crisis of confidence was of course directed towards President Lyndon B. Johnson who Robert Kennedy attacked regarding the war in Vietnam. At this event, Kennedy acknowledged that he had been part of many of the early decisions regarding events in Vietnam. He stated that during his brother's administration the South Vietnamese government, which they supported, was "riddled with corruption, inefficiency and greed," adding,

> If that is the case, as it may well be, then I am willing to bear my share of the responsibility, before my fellow citizens. But past error is no excuse for its own perpetration. Tragedy is a tool for the living to gain wisdom . . . Now, as ever, we do ourselves best justice when we measure ourselves against ancient tests, as in Sophocles: 'All men make mistakes, but a good man yields when he knows his course is wrong, and he repairs the evil.' The only sin, he said, is pride.[17]

Robert Kennedy apologized for his part in the growth of United States involvement in Indochina and had come to realize the error of his ways. He refused to remain a part of what he saw as a doomed war in Asia. His speech received large cheers from a young audience that writer Thurston Clark stated were perhaps appreciating an adult that could admit to a mistake or even because they had once supported the war and Kennedy's "mea culpa" made it easier for them to admit that they too had been wrong.[18] Our leaders must admit when they have made a mistake on policy. Americans must not judge them harshly, but rather look at them as humans that make mistakes and are not overcome with pride.

The George W. Bush administration has refused to admit wrongdoing, and has continued to be entrenched with their arrogant pride and sustained a war that remains immoral and useless. Robert Kennedy's actions are a measure of human character and are an example of how this nation today lacks the moral leadership that Kennedy embodied and now desperately needs. Our nation today is bleeding with the stab wounds of war and discontent. Our need of assistance is not forthcoming and while our government and president remain overcome with arrogance and unwilling to apply the proper help, it is our society that will suffer the ramifications of their conceit.

At the onset of the Vietnam War Robert Kennedy believed that the American people were willing to accept what the government was telling them about the war. In the early years of the fighting they did nothing when newspapers and news station reports brought the Vietnam War into their civilian homes. As the fighting grew worse and the death toll rose, people began to speak out against the war and looked to Robert Kennedy for support in the anti-war movement. He viewed the war as a slaughter, because he felt that the war was nothing more than another example of the scale that violence could inflict on innocent people. The war was treachery and it was unjust. In Kennedy's argument, the war in Vietnam needed to stop and with its termination would be an end to the deaths of innocent Vietnamese and Americans.

In that same sense, Kennedy probably feared of the desensitizing of the American people through the visions of violence that were presented to them. The effects of watching actual violence can be depressing and the longer an individual watches it the more numb they become to its terror. This is not unlike the state of America in 2008. The country blindly moved forward after the attacks on the World Trade Center and Pentagon on September 11, 2001. Society ushered in the new millennium with a new understanding of horror and since that day no American arguably has been the same. As a student, I watched on television as both the North and South Towers of the World Trade Center fell. I watched the horror of people jumping out of buildings, the fear on peoples faces as news story after news bulletin created more fear and panic. I remember being told the White House was on fire, that Air Force One was under attack. It read like something out of an episode of *24* and if I had watched the show at that time, I would have wished for Jack Bauer to come and save the day. The truth of the matter is this all happened. The White House and Air Force One were safe, but it is still an example of the level of fear that took place among average citizens in a moment of disaster. The visions of this event are entrenched in my memory and will never be forgotten. I think most people that were aware of their surroundings in September of 2001 see incredible differences between the years before the terrorist attacks and the years since.

After September of 2001, there was a strong desire and need for retaliation. The entire country wanted to find the people that perpetuated this heinous crime and go after them. People wanted to bring them to justice, and make them pay for what they did. At the same time that the country banded together in anger, the nation also came together in hope and understanding. For the first time in along time, maybe since before the 1960s, the United States felt as if it lived up to the term "united." People began to show a new appreciation for politics, nationalism, and were prideful in togetherness with fellow Americans. Even other countries that at one time had been called enemies to democracy and world freedom, were now called friends in the world's newest struggle against global terrorism. In 2001, I was a young adult at the age of nineteen and like many of my countrymen was overcome with a sense of patriotism. I looked at the promise the United States had at that time in becoming an instrument to develop lasting peace around the world. For an instant it looked as if, the world would band together in the aftermath of horror and in its shadow create a world and society dedicated to harmony. The unfortunate reality of this hope was the realization that this was merely chalk on a watery board. In the blink of an eye all of this hope was gone. The interesting thing about violence is that when used as a tool of revenge it is, as Albert Schweitzer, winner of the 1952 Nobel Peace Prize, once stated, like a "rolling stone, which, when a man hath forced up a hill, will return upon him with greater violence, and break those bones whose sinews gave it motion."[19]

Of course some might look at a statement such as "world peace" with trepidation and speculation, because many have tried to accomplish this before and have failed. Even so, I felt that the world might actually band together in a major struggle against tyranny and in the end the world organization would triumph. For a time, this hope lived on. America invaded Afghanistan attacking Al-Qaeda at every corner, going after Osama Bin Laden, the man that had orchestrated the September 11th attacks. It even seemed for a time that America was winning. As days turned into weeks and weeks turned into months, the growing nationalism that had developed in the weeks after September 11th started to dwindle and then fade.

Then in 2003, a report was issued stating that it was probable, from a high level of intelligence, that Iraq had been a knowing accomplice in the September 11th attacks and now should be the next step in the Global War on Terrorism. As other reports and intelligence also concluded, Iraq had Weapons of Mass Destruction (WMD), and therefore was a potential threat to the world. Yet many parts of the world felt very different about Iraq's role in regards to September 11th, as well as whether or not they had "Weapons of Mass Destruction." The United States would use this intelligence, refuse to acknowledge the necessity of the United Nations, and use a preemptive strike to invade Iraq in 2003 leaving many nations to distrust American leadership. France who had sent troops to Afghanistan in support of the American War on Terror refused to acknowledge America's need to attack Iraq based on its information. The price of their questioning America's refusal to wait for the United Nations to act was to be perceived and labeled in the American media as being traitors.[20]

Today, it has become evident that Iraq did not have WMD's and was not an accomplice with Al-Qaeda, the group that had attacked the United States on September 11th.[21] Some Americans still today feel that Iraq did have something to do with September 11th, yet no evidence can confirm that claim.[22] Still, Americans watch as news report after news report brings the War for Iraqi Freedom into American homes, and senselessly watch as the war in Iraq drags the image of America through the mud. In 2003, I believed the invasion of Iraq to be the wrong move and thought disobeying the United Nations seriously jeopardized that organizations power on a world stage. In 2003, and still today, I believed that with the attack on Iraq the credibility of the United States as a major world power had and has been compromised.

But, what can be done? The White House was wrong with its stance regarding Iraq, and the fact that the president stood on an Air Force carrier declaring "Mission Accomplished," yet, in 2008, Americans still fight this unpopular and highly illogical war, is something to be ashamed of. America did not learn from history or from its mistakes. Robert Kennedy's words had warned generations about this and his stance regarding Vietnam's influence on his generation should have been enough of a "warning" not to get involved in Iraq. Either way, America invaded Iraq and are still there in 2008, a terrible mistake that has cost the country billions of dollars, credibility in the world, deaths of American military soldiers, deaths of Iraqi civilians, has actually increased terrorist cells in Iraq, has divided the country to an extent not seen since the 1960s, and made the world even worse than before September 11th. And what about the man that orchestrated the September 11th, attacks on the United States? He has not been caught.

Vietnam and Iraq, both unpopular wars in their own generations, but how future generations view what has taken place, will be open for debate and discussion. One thing is certain, the same type of war that Kennedy was living through and which he stood up and preached against, is the same type of war taking place and staining the American image now. Therefore, from his words and reflections, one can learn a vast abundance of information, which will help us cope and understand the world Americans live in today. Through his words on violence and what he felt enhanced cruelty, one gets the sense that America need only look in a mirror to see the image of his warning. Violence was the essence of Vietnam and has become the essence of the war in Iraq. Different enemies, yet violence in both events becomes the ultimate winner. Even more worrisome, is that both wars have the ability to reach from Iraq or Vietnam and grab you in your chair in Boston, Massachusetts.

Robert Kennedy continued his speech moving to his next point to hammer home regarding how violence has creped into people's homes without them even realizing it. He discussed,

We glorify killing on movie and television screens and call it entertainment.

How desensitized will young Americans become with the amount of violence that is presented on television? Whether it is the footage of the war in Iraq or countless movies and television shows that are on each and everyday, images of violence are all around us. Americans must also remember that just because hate and violence are all around us, does not mean that there is a complete lack of love around us. Love, as well as hope is there, if even hidden slightly. The job is to make love more noticeable and easily defined. This can be done with an attack on violence, because there is no better poison against hate than love. Leaving the example of Iraq, let us now shift our attention to the idea of violence on television and movies and even in today's society, violence in video games.

There have been many movies that people have paid to watch on the big screen or purchased on DVD that are examples of violent entertainment. People watch movies and become entranced and in some cases infatuated with the most violent of characters. In many movies violence is presented on a scale never seen on the big screen before. There is evidence of this in movies like Saw or Hostel, where victims are chopped up and other forms of pain inflicted. All of these images are used in the form of entertainment, yet at the same time they are disturbing. I believe that Robert Kennedy witnessed the beginning of an age of television where day in and day out people could turn on their televisions and watch movies with violent themes.

Robert Kennedy felt that society was already violent enough, and the real violence needed to end, so putting that violent behavior on television was taking a step in the wrong direction. Too often aggression and murder are glorified on television, and with that allowance, people become accustomed to the idea of cruelty. People hear of news reports of violence and the horrible things that take place, yet are not surprised because they have became familiar with that type of violence. Because of this people become desensitized to the violence that they are watching and may try to imitate what they witnessed. This is a growing concern for American children. The American Academy of Children and Psychiatry published the following statement in 2002,

> American children watch an average of three to fours hours of television daily. Television can be a powerful influence in developing value systems and shaping behavior. Unfortunately, much of today's television programming is violent. Hundreds of studies of the effects of TV violence on children and teenagers have found that children may: become 'immune' or numb to the horror of violence, gradually accept violence as a way to solve problems, imitate the violence they observe on television; and identify with certain characters, victims and/or victimizers.[23]

They continued,

> Extensive viewing of television violence by children causes greater aggressiveness. Sometimes, watching a single violent program can increase aggressiveness. Children who view shows in which violence is very realistic, frequently repeated or unpunished, are more likely to imitate what they see. Children with emotional, behavioral, learning or impulse control problems may be more easily influenced by TV violence. The impact of TV violence may be immediately evident in the child's behavior or may surface years later. Young people can even be affected when the family atmosphere shows no tendency toward violence.[24]

Not only is real violence enough, the type of violence being portrayed on television can have a lasting and catastrophic effect on impressionable children. Along these same lines, especially in today's society, many people are looking into a correlation between violence and video games.

As one article read, "Researchers at the Indiana University School of Medicine said that brain scans of kids who played a violent video game showed an increase in emotional arousal—and a corresponding decrease of activity in brain areas involved in self-control, inhibition and attention."[25] The American Psychological Association (APA) published in April of 2000 in their *Journal of Personality and Social Psychology* stated that playing violent video games "like Doom, Wolfenstein 3D or Mortal Kombat can increase a person's aggressive thoughts, feelings and behavior both in laboratory settings and in actual life."[26] Psychologists Craig A. Anderson, Ph.D. and Karen E. Dill, Ph.D. stated the following,

> One study reveals that young men who are habitually aggressive may be especially vulnerable to the aggression-enhancing effects of repeated exposure to violent games . . . the other study reveals that even a brief exposure to violent

video games can temporarily increase aggressive behavior in all types of partic-
ipants.[27]

Many people have even made attempts to legally bring companies that make
these violent video games to court, believing that the level of violence in
these games can lead to murder. As a March 6, 2005 article read,

> Imagine if the entertainment industry created a video game in which you could
> decapitate police officers, kill them with a sniper rifle, massacre them with a
> chainsaw, and set them on fire. Think anyone would buy such a violent game?
> They would, and they have. The game Grand Theft Auto has sold more than 35
> million copies, with worldwide sales approaching $2 billion. Two weeks ago, a
> multi-million dollar lawsuit was filed in Alabama against the makers and mar-
> keters of Grand Theft Auto, claiming that months of playing the game led a
> teenager to go on a rampage and kill three men, two of them police officers.[28]

What studies have shown is that the level of violence on television and in
video games can desensitize people. This will cause them to suffer from a
lack of understanding on the reality of what they are viewing and playing.
This is the same type of desensitization that Kennedy warned could happen if
people refused to accept that what they watched on television was a perversion of reality.

With all of that being said, other countries with less violent tendencies play
the same video games and watch the same movies as the United States. As
Michael Moore, tried to figure out in his award winning documentary, *Bowling
for Columbine*, what is it about the United States that allows many to commit
such violent acts against society, especially shootings in American schools? As
he concluded it cannot be because American history has a violent past. It is easily understood that many other countries have just as much if not more of a violent past than America. They all watch the same movies and play the same
video games, so what is it about America that makes it have more violent acts,
easily more gun deaths, against our public than any other country. Interestingly
enough, Michael Moore, had trouble finding his answer. He found that the one
thing America is obsessed with is fear. People are afraid of their neighbors and
afraid of what is unknown. This fear leads them to unpredictable conclusions
and Americans then find themselves creating a society that lacks a clear appreciation of reason. When it comes to the need to find out why Americans are so
violent, the solution is not in finding the answer to why things happen, like
Robert Kennedy discussed in his speech, but rather to bring awareness to a
growing problem and come together to promote change.

While television does have violence on the screen, citizens should realize
that the point of television and movies is entertainment. Although one might
disagree with the amount of violence on television, there is an "on off" switch

on the box, so that one does not have to watch it. In this case it is up to the individual themselves, or parents if the individual is a child, to turn off the television if something is violent. One must take accountability for their own actions when it comes to what they watch or allow their children to watch.

Kennedy moved forward with his discussion about violence on television by providing the next trigger to his point,

> *We make it easy for men of all shades of sanity to acquire whatever weapons and ammunition they desire.*

This statement also coincides with his previous comments. If society numbs people's feelings towards violence or the basic principles of morality, then allowing them access to weapons is a deadly combination. Access is easy for all types of Americans to actually obtain many types of weaponry. With the Virginia Tech shooter, he was able to buy one of his guns off the internet. This is a clear breakdown in our society and is an example of why there is a need for stricter gun control laws. Yet, still Americans can buy their weapons online and can own many types of weapons that have no place in the hands of average citizens.

Why do Americans have the ability to own assault-weapons? What is the moral need of owning one? As I stated before I have serious doubts that it is needed to hunt. I understand that many will point to the fact that it is their constitutional right, written in the Second Amendment. Although I disagree with their interpretation of the amendment, I will not argue the constitutionality of it, but understand that hunting is legal and the law is the law. Even if one believes in the need to be allowed to own guns, they still see the need of serious gun control. Weapons of any kind should not be allowed into the hands of the wrong person. Society would not allow nuclear capabilities to fall into the hands of the wrong people that have no business possessing nuclear weapons. Therefore, even at home on American soil there should be a need to make sure that the people that should not own guns are not allowed access to them. This can only be done with stricter gun control laws. I am not saying take away all guns from all people, but rather to restrict the types of weapons that Americans can own and who has access to them. With strict gun control laws, people that have the right to own certain weapons maintain that right, but those that should not have access to them lose access to this serious possession and potentially the problem is averted.

Young children that kill students should not have access to weapons or ammunition. That is a simple cut and dry fact. Children should not be able to gain access to an arsenal of weaponry and be able to, with that access, bring it to school and bring violence to a place of learning where students need to feel safe. Robert Kennedy witnessed the need to have greater gun control laws, because of a growing fear, especially in the 1960s, of having weapons getting into the hands of the wrong people. Yet still, in 2004 Americans allowed a major piece of the "Brady Bill" to expire and still today in 2008, the wrong types of people are gaining access to weaponry and thus able to keep the level of violence at a heightened level. In an even harsher reality, those families that do have guns in the house, must take a greater responsibility in keeping those guns where children will never be able to find them.

School children today, like in the 1950s and 1960s, have drills to alert them of danger. These are not normal fire drills, but drills that require students to take action if a student has a gun in the school. In all reality, the ability of students possessing guns should be able to be stopped. One could easily say that schools should have more security, more metal detectors, more security cameras, but in all seriousness that is not a permanent solution. It can only eliminate part of the problem through a temporary resolution. Soon people forget the necessity of this enforcement and the system itself begins to breakdown. Once people forget, the system slacks off, violence again creeps in and history repeats itself. There is a need for a permanent solution to this growing crisis. The only permanent solution can be education, stricter gun laws and an ambitious political force intent on curbing the level of violence in society.

This level of violence should not be tolerated and must be stopped with political and moral will, something the United States has lacked in recent years. Kennedy continued his speech with harsher truths,

> *Too often we honor swagger and bluster and wielders of force; too often we excuse those who are willing to build their own lives on the shattered dreams of others.*

In the long history of the world society has honored those individuals that succeeded in making a lasting contribution to history. One individual that I personally have become intrigued about in recent years is William Wilberforce. I spoke of him earlier and his dedication to the abolition of slavery in Great Britain and the destruction of the international slave trade all around the globe. He was a remarkable man with all the virtues and ambitions that make him an important figure of world history. He is in history perhaps one of the best known of all abolitionists in a world that has created few. While watching a movie detailing Wilberforce's fight to abolish slavery, there was a line at the end of the film that made me think of the line by Robert Kennedy that was included in his "Mindless Menace of Violence" speech.

In the movie there was a speech given by an actor portraying Lord Charles Fox regarding the success of Wilberforce in ending slavery in Great Britain. He said the following,

> When people speak of great men, they think of men like Napoleon—men of violence. Rarely do they think of peaceful men. But by contrast the reception they

will receive when they return home from their battles. Napoleon will arrive in pomp and in power, a man who's achieved the very summit of earthly ambition. And yet his dreams will be haunted by the oppressions of war. William Wilberforce, however, will return to his family, lay his head on his pillow and remember: the slave trade is no more.[29]

In history Napoleon is viewed as a conquering military hero, who like the actor said reached the pinnacle of worldly success. Yet, all too often in history people forget about the individuals that had just as much ambition and drive and, were more so, dedicated to sound and moral principles. Americans honor the great military hero's, yet stumble over the stories of regular politicians, abolitionists, and common individuals who played instrumental roles in bringing about change in society. As Kennedy believed, society honors the swagger and arrogance that comes with military victories and watch military documentaries and movies, in the end feeling immense patriotism and glory. It is not incorrect to honor and respect those leaders, but at the same time it is wrong to only focus on their conquests and not on the ambitions of the citizenry or the foundation of those leaders work. Many times the needs of the state and the power of the leader used their force to build their empire on the hopes and dreams of other societies. Many times, the citizenry of their own state were abandoned and their rights abused. People excuse these acts of violence against innocence because the ends seem to justify the means. Yet, no matter what empires have been built on the "shattered dreams" and ambitions of its people or others, there is something valuable that is almost assuredly lost.

Not long ago, I wrote a book titled, *Martyr to Freedom: The Life and Death of Captain Daniel Drayton.* It discusses the life of an unknown abolitionist that gave the greater portion of his life trying to speak out and help slaves in the United States. I found his tale interesting because he was a man that lived his life dedicated to the belief that all men were created equal under the laws of nature and state. He believed in freedom, he believed in humanity. Yet, his life was an example of failure because everything he tried to do ended with him in dismay and unconnected from those around him. In the end, Daniel Drayton took his own life at the age of fifty five. Although tragic and complicated, Drayton lived an extraordinary life. He can be classified as one of those individuals, like Wilberforce, that dreamed with their eyes wide open. They are the ones that witnessed unethical actions and went forth amongst society trying to bring civility out of chaos. These men had ambition that is worth more in its essence than any success a military or political leader could ever possess. So, while society honors the "pomp" of many past figures remember that there are others that deserve just as much respect, and Robert Kennedy is most assuredly an individual that deserves recognition for righteous reasons.

His dedication to the poor, the less able, African American rights, his fight against an unjust war, and his ability to see the beauty in everyday life and the need to preserve the magnificence of life, is why Robert Kennedy's vision is timeless. He lived for others, rather than living for himself. These are the types of men that should be honored, and it is not for military conquest. Rather society should respect them because of what their lives were dedicated to. Of course, the pages of history can go on and on detailing the amount of people that should be respected because of their ambition, and I think that most Americans can gain something from this new perspective of historical interpretation.

Robert Kennedy continued,

Some Americans who preach non-violence abroad fail to practice it here at home.

America is a place of peace and freedom. But in all reality, America has had a difficult time practicing what it has preached. During World War II, the nation vilified the Nazi regime for the atrocities committed during the Holocaust, and was correct in doing so. Yet, at the same time, while the United States placed itself upon a pedestal of human rights, African Americans were treated as second class citizens, even subjected to segregation in the armed forces. While the Americans liberated Europe from the clutches of a tyrannical ruler and took on not only the Germans but also the Japanese, the nation's leaders placed regular Americans that were of Japanese descent in American concentration camps.[30] America did this through Franklin D. Roosevelt's Executive Order 9066. These camps in no way shape or form, resembled the Nazi concentration camps, but what it did show was a sense of racial prejudice and misunderstandings present at that time. The government took action against a single group based on who they were. As far as I know, there were no containment camps for Germans living in the United States.

The United States has always been a nation devoted to human rights and non-violence, yet as Robert Kennedy viewed it at that time, the country was waging an unjust and unpopular war bringing violence to American soldiers that were dying unnecessarily. In the 1960s, as well as decades before and since, the United States has demanded that other nations respect the rights and privileges of its own citizens. Yet at the same time, the United States refused to respect the rights of its own citizens. For a century after the inception of the thirteenth, fourteenth, and fifteenth Amendments, African Americans were still refused the simple basic rights granted to all Americans simply because they were born with a darker skin. Jim Crow laws were enacted in the South and the court case *Plessey vs. Ferguson* created the doctrine of "separate but equal." Poll Tax, literacy tests and the "grandfather clause" were used throughout the South to deny African Americans their right to vote.[31]

In 1968, Robert Kennedy spoke of the world he perceived around him and the country he felt had made several missteps in its treatment of those perceived as lesser citizens. He witnessed how America had refused to live up to the Constitution, and went to war with another country to contain communism and spread the ideal of democracy. Even after Kennedy was dead, his message of non-violence went unabated, with the nation witnessing President Richard Nixon begin a bombing campaign against Cambodia, a neutral country. In all reality, Robert Kennedy's message has never died and is as strong today as it was in 1968 and as fresh as the ink he used to write it. Americans live in a free and democratic society in the United States of America in 2008, and the principles that this country stands for are virtuous and absolute. Whether it is education, health care, or other social programs, American citizens in many instances are not allowed access to needed services. It is possible that my anger over this situation is bias. I am a history professor at Roger Williams University and Bristol Community College and understand the absolute need to have an informed citizenry. I am also an American that has, in the past, had difficulty being able to afford health care and have seen much of my money go to paying the costs of this crucial care. I also have a heart and have difficulty looking into the eyes of a man that has to live on the street or a woman that suffers from a major skin aliment but cannot afford the five thousand dollar shots every other week. In the end, I love the United States of America and want to be proud of its message and how it protects its citizens. I want the world to look at the United States as an example of how a nation grows successful because of the ability of all its citizens.

One "practice what you preach" issue that Kennedy would be ashamed to see today is the country's stance on the use of torture in interrogations. In a "post-9/11" world the government has seen it fit to avoid a stance on the issue of torture and unfortunately, for the reputation of this country, it has come to fruition that the military has used torture techniques while interrogating suspected terrorists. No matter who the suspect is and no matter what crime they have supposedly committed, there is no way in a free society and a nation based on a living constitution that the use of torture is ever acceptable. There were several Republican candidates that ran for the 2008 presidential nomination that refused to take a stance on torture. To refuse to say whether or not they would approve the use of torture, as president of the United States of America, is a serious misstep in American foreign and political policy. The results of this miscalculation could seriously jeopardize America's position in the world. To think that someone could become a president of the United States and approve the use of torture is outrageous, immoral, and highly illegal on the international stage. John McCain, Senator from Arizona, and Republican presidential candidate for 2008, has come out strongly against the use of torture. This is not surprising since McCain was tortured as a prisoner during the Vietnam War. So therefore who do the American people listen to on this issue? Do they listen to those with a political and personal agenda regarding the use of an immoral tactic? Or do they look to someone that was inflicted by the same pain, which they seek to eradicate from American thought?

Another problem with the idea of torture is not only that it is illegal and immoral, but also what it does for the safety of American men and women in uniform all over the globe. To approve torture, means throwing international law out the window and installing a new American initiative that other countries will assuredly follow. If the United States uses torture, then other nations will use torture, and the dominos will continue to fall. This is not a path the United States wants to travel down. There is a reason that torture is outlawed in the world. It is to protect prisoners captured in combat. To change that approach to international law, is a clear path to further violence, and most assuredly will breed retaliation. If there is hope in the world to further curtail the use of violence and the perversion of violence, then America must stand strong and tall as a beacon for the world, not as a hypocrite, but rather as a nation that practices what it preaches.

If America can finally take that initiative, which it has not done during the present administration, then there is hope that the image of the United States that is so vilified in the world at this time will begin to heal. But, that dirty image will never wash away or be clean if the country backs illegal measures and continues to act as a bully in the world. Kennedy then moved forward with his speech to include the next line. He stated,

Some who accuse others of inciting riots have by their own conduct invited them.

Kennedy has linked these passages together because they go together in their overall objective. He discussed the use of double standards in policies. On the one hand, America has acted as a bully not practicing what it has preached in the world. On the other hand, he accused those that attack others for inciting riots, yet they themselves are to blame for creating the very problems that are causing the demonstrators to riot. This was a time when African Americans were struggling to gain their rights and protections under the law. Even after the law took their side, there were still many places that refused to respect their basic rights as American citizens. Riot after riot occurred in America in the 1960s, especially in 1968, and were started in opposition to the lack of support by the government, especially political leaders in the South, about the rights of the people.

Whether it was the war in Vietnam, civil rights, or student rights, and more, Kennedy perceived that these riots were not the actions of a mob, but rather had been invited by the inaction of the government and improper use of federal, state, and local power. The conduct of the government invited these riots, and therefore blame should not be placed on the people for demonstrating, if they do so peacefully. Rather the government needs to take a long look in the mirror to find the underlining problem that was bringing people to the streets. If they wanted the violence to end, they needed to stop their own use of violence in keeping the rights away from those that demanded them. It was subtle, but Kennedy made his point. Although not condoning the violence of riots, he believed that in order to stop the violence one cannot use more violence. Instead what was needed was the ability to work out these problems though peace and progress.

While Kennedy discussed this point about double standards taking over American social and political life, he set the stage for his next statement. He stated,

Some look for scapegoats, others look for conspiracies, but this much is clear: violence breeds violence, repression brings retaliation, and only a cleansing of our whole society can remove this sickness from our soul.

One of the most powerful statements, among many, in this speech is the declaration listed above. I personally like Kennedy's statement, about how in American society people "look for scapegoats, others look for conspiracies." This is so true in American society. Americans love the concept of the conspiracy. When I was young, it must have been around 1993, which would have made me eleven, I watched the film *JFK* by Oliver Stone, which starred Kevin Costner. It was a very fascinating movie and very entertaining. I watched the film and was engrossed by the powerful message that it was conveying, John F. Kennedy had been killed, not by Lee Harvey Oswald, but rather it was the United States government that was behind his assassination. The movie portrayed how the District Attorney of New Orleans, Jim Garrison, uncovered evidence and testimony that pointed to as high up as Lyndon B. Johnson in a conspiracy to kill the sitting president, John F. Kennedy. As a young impressionable adolescent, I took the movie, foolishly, as fact.

As an instructor of American history, my courses do an assignment that requires them to watch a Hollywood film and then research the history behind the interpretation given. I have my students do what I call a "Fact or Fiction" research paper. It is their assignment to watch a Hollywood film that is "based on a true story," and then research the actual event the movie is portraying. So for example, I would have them watch the movie *Bobby* and investigate what took place the day Robert Kennedy was killed, using primary and secondary sources. The student's job would be to reconstruct the film, by discussing what the movie added in for purely entertainment value, and what was factually correct. It is astounding the lengths that Hollywood will go in depicting history, yet keeping it "based on true story." I tell my students, everyone should understand that the purpose of Hollywood is entertainment and not to be historians. But, when I was eleven, I did not understand that concept and when I watched *JFK* I thought it was entirely true. Much to my embarrassment when I got older and the teacher in my middle school history course said that Lee Harvey Oswald had killed the president and I raised my hand to say he was wrong. It was LBJ.

For one thing, as a professor, I have learned you never argue with your teacher, and also it is ok to watch movies "based on a true story" and understand that the concept is based on real events, but if someone wants the whole story they must research it themselves. This leads me to my overall point about conspiracy theories. The movie *JFK* uses more than anything else, the countless conspiracy theory books written about the assassination for its theme, and therefore although based on an actual event it is based more on opinion than actual fact. Why then are there so many books written about the John F. Kennedy assassination that feel so strongly that it was not a lone assassin, but rather an orchestrated attempt to sidestep the American political spectrum? It is because America has a fascination with the idea of the conspiracy. Again, in my courses I have my students at one point in the last half of the semester investigate different conspiracies and see what they are about and why people believe in them. One would be surprised and "entertained" by the evidence that is uncovered and investigated.

I have had my students investigate some of the most popular conspiracy theories in today's society. Some of the theories that my students have investigated have been the TWA Flight 800—Did a fuel jet explode or was it by a missile? New Coke Conspiracy—Did the Coca-Cola Company really fake a mistake to become very wealthy? Moon Landing—Was it a great move forward in exploration of the solar system or a great hoax created on a sound set? These are just a few of the many conspiracy theories that are discussed in American society as well as investigated by my students. Now, the most important question then is what is a conspiracy? By definition,

> A conspiracy theory attempts to attribute the ultimate cause of an event or chain of events, usually political, social, or historical events, or the concealment of such causes from public knowledge, to a secret, and often deceptive, plot by a covert alliance of powerful or influential people or organizations.[32]

Now the term "conspiracy theory" is used by many of today's best scholars and in popular culture to identity what can be considered folklore, especially an explanatory narrative which is constructed with particular methodological flaws.[33] In the most part, especially today, conspiracy theories lack readily

verifiable evidence, which in great part is why they are not always taken seriously by most people.

So with our definition of what a conspiracy and a conspiracy theory are, why
are Americans fascinated by them? For one thing, conspiracy theories are often
preferred by individuals as a way to understand what is happening around them
without having to grasp the complexities of history and political interaction.[34]
People need to believe that things happen for a reason and it could not have
been as simple or as clear cut as the evidence suggest. Most Americans believe
John F. Kennedy was the victim of a conspiracy and the evidence against Oswald was fabricated. In that same respect the evidence supporting a conspiracy
is unreliable and most evidence presented since the assassination has been dis-
proved. Still, Americans believe that the conspiracy is real. It is because people
need to believe that what happened, especially to John F. Kennedy, was bigger
than just the work of one man. People need to believe a man with such talent,
who people had such hope in and was seen as an important figure, had to have
been taken down by something bigger than us, as well as him.

The idea of the conspiracy lives on in American culture, with no end in
sight. Kennedy, who had seen his brother killed and then saw the growth of
conspiracy theories surrounding his death and scapegoats, knew that it does
not change the result. What is done is done and nothing can change what history has already written. The violence perpetrated has already struck. The
need to find improvable and unrealistic answers helps no one. In the end, violence cannot be cured through blame, but rather by moving forward in pro-
moting change.

Robert Kennedy believed that hostility could not be cured with more violence and the country had seen too many instances of how violence only
breeds more violence. When a person is abused enough he will retaliate
against his oppressor. Robert Kennedy, as he watched the civil rights movement unfold, knew that if African Americans and other minorities were oppressed by the government, they would petition the government for change.
Seeing how violence was used to combat their protests, he knew the next step
would be retaliation from the oppressed portion of society. It is quite obvious
that this is not a racial issue, it is not a gender issue, and it is not a cultural issue, rather it is an ethical issue. Anyone in this world would not take too
kindly to being repressed, especially in a free and democratic society. In the
1960s, minorities, with African Americans at the helm, were being repressed
from education, work, school, public life, the simple basic necessities of
transportation or dining, and this type of repression was sure to create retaliation from a group wanting to break free from the chains of bondage. This
was exactly what took place in the 1960s with the demonstrations, riots, sit-
ins, and other forms of disobedience in American society at that time.

Kennedy witnessed what took place and offered up an explanation of why these things were taking place.

For Robert Kennedy the only way to stop the path of the storm was to redirect it. Instead of allowing the violence to ensue, discuss why the violence happened in the first place and move forward. I think that everyone can understand that the use of force is never a single option and the use of violence will never be met with open acceptance. In 1968, Kennedy felt the country had come to a stand still with the level of violence inflicted on society as a whole. When he stated, "only a cleansing of our whole society can remove this sickness from our soul," he was offering a chance to begin anew. With a new change of guard, the country could finally live up to its obligations, its character, and its beliefs. He felt the country, especially since the assassination of his brother, had lost its way. Policies, violence, and war, everything began to stain the image of the nation he loved. This speech in the light of the death of Martin Luther King Jr. was a chance to send a message to the people of the United States. He wanted to convey to them that the times in which they lived did not have to be so chaotic and sad. Through his speech he painted a picture of what was wrong and how the good of human nature could still prevail.

In the backdrop of the violence that took Martin Luther King Jr., Kennedy used that opportunity to discuss the emptiness left behind by something man made. The cleansing of society is the rebuilding and reconstructing of the American way and for many the rebuilding of the American dream. To be able to send one's child to school without the fear of being shot, to go shopping at a mall without the fear of a sniper, to be a women alone without the fear of being raped, to be human and have the ambition to conquer one's hopes and dreams. This is the cleansing that Robert Kennedy speaks of then, and a cleansing that is needed now.

Violence is a sickness, it is a disease, it is not however a virus that is incurable. America simply needs to understand and recognize the symptoms, and then find a proper solution. Robert Kennedy in the first half of his speech on violence provided future generations not only with the tools to combat violence but reasons why it has continued to progress. Although a 1968 speech, in 2008 this speech has transcended time and has just as much a powerful meaning today as it did then. It is interesting what the world would be like if people did not have to fear. Of course, is this peaceful world possible? That I cannot say for certain, but the alternative that is filled with fear, is worth the leap. It is important and vital that during the journey of life, which everyone goes through, along the way one turns around and reflect at the growth that has been accomplished. Remember, you never know how far you have gone unless you turn around every once and a while. Each of us can move to change the world, and our journey makes us who we are. As John O'Hurley eloquently stated, "make the leap and the net will appear."

NOTES

1. Thurston Clarke, "The Heartbreak Campaign," *Vanity Fair*, June 2008.

2. Clarke, "The Heartbreak Campaign."

3. Clarke, "The Heartbreak Campaign."

4. John O'Hurley, "2006 Providence College Commencement Address," (Address given at the Dunkin Donuts Center in Providence, Rhode Island on 21 May 2006). Providence College, Providence, Rhode Island.

5. Thomas Lawrence, *Seven Pillars of Wisdom* (New York: Wordsworth Editions Limited, 1997), 7.

6. O'Hurley, "2006 Providence College Commencement Address," 21 May 2006.

7. O'Hurley, "2006 Providence College Commencement Address," 21 May 2006.

8. Associated Press, "Police: 10 month old Pittsburg baby dies after rape, assault," *Associated Press*, 11 November 2007, <www.wpxi.com/news/ 14636292/detail.html ?rss =burg&psp=news> (18 January 2008).

9. Associated Press, "Police: 10 month old Pittsburg baby dies after rape, assault," *Associated Press*, 11 November 2007, <www.wpxi.com/news/ 14636292/detail.htm l?rss =burg&psp=news> (18 January 2008).

10. Allan Chernoff and Brian Vitagliano, "Philadelphia Mom Bought Guns for Boy," *CNN.com*, 12 October 2007, <www.cnn.com/2007/US/10/12/ student.arsenal/ index.html> (15 October 2008).

11. Karen O'Connor and Larry J. Sabato, *Essential of American Government: Continuity and Change* (Boston: Pearson Longman, 2008), 70, 121.

12. Associated Press, "Man Opens Fire in Omaha Mall, Killing 8 before Committing Suicide," *USA Today.com*, 5 December 2007, <www.kval.com/ news/national/12170681.html> (20 December 2008).

13. Linda Thompson, "Police Identify Guneman as 18-year-old Bosnian," *Desert News.com*, 16 February 2007, <www.deseretnews.com/ dn/view/0,1249,660195221, 00.html> (17 February 2008).

14. Anderson, *The Sixties*, 101.

15. Anderson, 101–102.

16. Clarke, "The Heartbreak Campaign."

17. Clarke, "The Heartbreak Campaign."

18. Clarke, "The Heartbreak Campaign."

19. Albert Schweitzer, *Quotes*, 2008, <http://www.schweitzer.org/> (8 June 2008).

20. Russell Brooker and Todd Schaefer, *Public Opinion in the 21st Century: Let the People Speak?* (Boston: Houghton Mifflin Company, 2006), 349–351.

21. Brooker, 316–318.

22. Brooker, 316–318.

23. "Children and TV Violence," *American Academy of Child & Adolescent Psychiatry*, *AACAP.com*, Number 13, November 2002, <www.aacap.org/cs/root/ facts_for_families/children _and_tv_violence> (5 June 2007).

24. "Children and TV Violence," *American Academy of Child & Adolescent Psychiatry*, *AACAP.com*, Number 13, November 2002, <www.aacap.org/cs/root/ facts_for_families/children _and_tv_violence> (5 June 2007).

25. Kristen Kalning, "Does Game Violence Make Teen Aggressive?" *MSNBC.Com*, 8 December 2006, <http://www.msnbc.msn.com/id/16099971/> (4 May 2007).

26. Karen E. Dill, "Violent Video Games Can Increase Aggression," *Journal of Personality and Social Psychology, APA.com,* 23 April 2000, <www.apa.org/releases/videogames.html> (5 June 2007).

27. Karen E. Dill, "Violent Video Games Can Increase Aggression," *Journal of Personality and Social Psychology, APA.com,* 23 April 2000, <www.apa.org/releases/videogames.html> (5 June 2007).

28. Associated Press, "Can a Video Game Lead to Murder?" *CBS News.com,* 6 March 2005, www.cbsnews.com/stories/2005/03/04/60minutes/main678261.shtml> (7 June 2007).

29. *Amazing Grace*, James Clayton and Micheal Apted, 117 minutes, Bristol Bay Productions, 2006, DVD.

30. David A. Horowitz, *On the Edge: The United States in the Twentieth Century* (United States: Thomson Wadsworth, 2005), 235.

31. Klinkner, *The Unsteady March,* 99 and 234.

32. *Merriam and Webster Dictionary and Thesaurus Online*, 2008, <http://www.merriam-webster.com/> (4 April 2008).

33. *Merriam and Webster Dictionary and Thesaurus Online*, 2008, <http://www.merriam-webster.com/> (4 April 2008).

34. Lev Grossman, "Why the 9/11 Conspiracy Theories won't go Away," Time.com, 3 September 2006, <www.time.com/time/magazine/article/0,9171,1531304,00.html> (12 October 2007).

Chapter Four

A Man among Men

It should be clear by now that a nation can be no stronger abroad than she is at home. Only an America which practices what it preaches about equal rights and social justice will be respected by those whose choice affects our future. Only an America which has fully educated its citizens is fully capable of tackling the complex problems and perceiving hidden dangers of the world in which we live.

—John F. Kennedy

Open up any world history text book and one will discover a history overwhelmed by violence and bursting at the seams with stories of individuals that have either been oppressed or subjected to some of the worst horrors imaginable. As a student at Providence College, I took a course titled "The Second World War." During this course students learned about everything imaginable about World War II. My peers and I learned not only about America's involvement in the war, but also looked at the war from a European standpoint. It was an extremely well balanced course and one of the most difficult courses I took as a graduate student. This course did a fantastic job in bringing in firsthand accounts of the war, providing it with a human feel. Information that one learns in college is fantastic, but nothing compares to the real life tale of horror, hope, and helplessness from someone that experienced the war for themselves. For one class during the semester our professor brought in a survivor of the Holocaust to speak to us. This gentleman, named Harold, would tell us the story of his life and his experience during the Nazi Holocaust.

Harold was born in Nuremberg, Germany and had two parents and one brother. During his early life he attended public school, played sports, and was treated as an equal. When Adolph Hitler and his Nazi Party came to power in 1933, things began to change and gradually the rights that he as a citizen had come to expect were being taken away from him. Harold was a German Jew. Thus, when the Nuremberg Decrees were instituted as law, people that had at one point called themselves his friend would assault him and even spit on him. It was at this point that Harold began to see the worst of human nature. By 1938, conditions grew worse. His rights were taken away and he needed to wear the Star of David on his clothes. By 1941, Harold was notified that he would be leaving Germany and be placed in forced labor camps. He was allowed just one suitcase and one blanket and then made the fifty hour trip to Latvia on a heavily armed Nazi train.

By December of 1941, the same month and year the Japanese attacked Pearl Harbor bringing the United States into the war, Harold felt demoralized and emotionally destroyed. He was hungry, with little rations of food, and behind his barracks at the camp, German military officers would use Jewish workers for target practice. He was even thrown in solitary confinement for a month. As he told us, it was reported that no Jew had ever survived such confinement. But he managed to hang on and live to see the guard open the door. For just under four years Harold went to different labor and extermination camps and his family, remarkably, was able to stay together. Then sadly at a new camp he was separated from his mother. While the audience listened, Harold told the story of his last vision of his mother. As he described how she was behind a fence, he became choked up and could not finish the story. That was the last time he ever saw his mother.

Although separated from his mother, he was still together with his brother and father. After almost four years in camps, he suddenly came down with typhoid and was sent to the infirmary. When the guards began to evacuate the camp and started to forcibly march everyone out, Harold was in fear that he would be executed, so he hid in a broken floor board under his barrack. For several days he stayed hidden in the floor until he heard the sound of tanks. When he came out of the floor, he was met by the United States Army. Harold had been saved by of all things typhoid, but his brother and father, whom he could not warn, were forced on the long march out of the camp. Harold never saw them again.

After being liberated by the United States, Harold had hoped to be able to find surviving members of his family, but with no luck. At a time when he believed he would never live to see the end of the war, he had survived and made it through one of the most horrendous acts of human evil. Harold is just one of millions that survived the Holocaust and his family is but three of six million that would perish at the hands of anti-Semitism.[1] One can imagine watching this man in his eighties telling this story. It moved the audience to tears. The level of violence, lack of empathy, and total disregard for human life, is one of the most disgusting instances in human history. Harold had survived, but the war cost him his family and left him forever scarred by the memories of those four years in Nazi camps. Listening to this survivor talk was a life changing experience. It showed how evil people can be, and yet how strong and compassionate others can act. Harold had helped other inmates and many had helped him. Sometimes in the worst of events, society pays witness to some of the best humanity has produced. The Second World War truly saw the worst and best that humanity has had to offer. As Prime Minister Winston Churchill stated in 1940,

> We have before us an ordeal of the most grievous kind. You ask, what is our policy? I say it is to wage war by land, sea and air—war with all our might and with all the strength God has given us—and to wage war against a monstrous tyranny never surpassed in the dark and lamentable catalogue of human crime. That is our policy.[2]

The Second World War witnessed the terror inflicted by Hitler, Mussolini, and the use of bombs of incredible power, but at the same time the war was an example of human compassion. It was an example of how action rather than indifference was used to help those in need.

One of the most notable survivors of the Holocaust is Elie Wiesel, awarded the 1986 Nobel Peace Prize for his fight against violence. He, like Harold, witnessed the sufferings of Jews in the Nazi concentration camps. As a teenager in Hungary, Elie Wiesel, along with his father, mother and sisters, were deported by the Nazis to Auschwitz extermination camp in occupied Poland.[3] While in Auschwitz, he was separated from his mother and younger sister, whom he never saw again. Wiesel and his father were then selected by German SS Dr. Josef Mengele for slave labor and found themselves at the nearby Buna rubber factory.[4] As one can only imagine their daily life included starvation, rations of soup and bread, brutal discipline, and a constant struggle against overwhelming despair. At one point, young Wiesel received twenty five lashes of the whip for a minor infraction.[5] As the Russian Army drew nearer to the camp, Wiesel and his father were moved to Buchenwald in Germany, where Wiesel's father died of starvation and exposure just before the camp was liberated by the Allies in 1945.[6]

One of the greatest speeches Elie Wiesel gave was at the Seventh White House Millennium Evening in Washington D.C., on April 12, 1999. The sad irony, this event would take place eight days prior to the Columbine shooting. Wiesel's speech was called "The Perils of Indifference," and it fits in very well with our discussion of Robert F. Kennedy's vision of violence in American society. When President Bill Clinton introduced Elie Wiesel he had the following words to say,

I never could have imagined that when the time finally came for him to stand in this spot and to reflect on the past century and the future to come, that we would be seeing children in Kosovo crowded into trains, separated from families, separated from their homes, robbed of their childhoods, their memories, their humanity.[7]

On April 20, 1999, the same day of the Columbine shooting, President Bill Clinton unleashed the largest bombing campaign of the Kosovo Conflict.[8] In over a one week span teenagers would unleash war on their school, President Clinton would unleash military fury on Kosovo and Elie Wiesel spoke of the many problems in America and around the world.

Elie Wiesel had this to say on the course of the new century and his thoughts on indifference,

What will the legacy of this vanishing century be? How will it be remembered in the new millennium? Surely it will be judged, and judged severely, in both moral and metaphysical terms. These failures have cast a dark shadow over humanity: two World Wars, countless civil wars, the senseless chain of assassinations—Gandhi, the Kennedy's, Martin Luther King, Sadat, Rabin—bloodbaths in Cambodia and Nigeria, India and Pakistan, Ireland and Rwanda, Eritrea and Ethiopia, Sarajevo and Kosovo; the inhumanity in the gulag and the tragedy of Hiroshima. And, on a different level, of course, Auschwitz and Treblinka. So much violence, so much indifference.[9]

Elie Wiesel was asking how history would judge the last century in human civilization. The wars, the assassinations, the genocides, and the violence all had left a terrible stain on history. He mentions Hiroshima, Rwanda, the deaths of political leaders and lastly the Nazi concentration camps, which he knew all too well. The last century will be judged on these terrible instances and each incident, according to Wiesel, was an act of indifference.

What is indifference? Etymologically, the word means 'no difference.' A strange and unnatural state in which the lines blur between light and darkness, dusk and dawn, crime and punishment, cruelty and compassion, good and evil. What are its courses and inescapable consequences? Can one possibly view indifference as a virtue? Is it necessary at times to practice it simply to keep one's sanity, live normally, enjoy a fine meal and a glass of wine, as the world around us experiences harrowing upheavals?[10]

Wiesel tried to define what it meant to be indifferent. He discussed how to be indifferent was to be neither bright nor dark. It is the line that blurs the opposite end of all spectrums. He asked what are the consequences of indifference and how can it be viewed from a societal standpoint?

In the end, Wiesel asked his listeners to ask themselves to interpret what indifference meant to them before he provides them with the reality that indifference creates. He even proposes a question of whether indifference can be used to keep one from losing their sanity in a time when there is so much horror in the world.

> Of course, indifference can be tempting—more than that, seductive. It is so much easier to look away from victims. It is so much easier to avoid such rude interruptions to our work, our dreams, our hopes. It is, after all, awkward, troublesome, to be involved in another person's pain and despair. Yet, for the person who is indifferent, his or her neighbor are of no consequence. And, therefore, their lives are meaningless. Their hidden or even visible anguish is of no interest. Indifference reduces the other to an abstraction.[11]

As Elie Wiesel discussed, to take part in the process of indifference can be very easily done and many times it is tempting. It is, as he said, much easier to look away and go about our daily routine without offensive interruption. To be involved in another person's pain and suffering, as Wiesel wants to make clear, is thought of as awkward and inappropriate. Indifference creates nothing and it destroys nothing. But it allows for the pain of the victim to remain and go unaddressed. Everyone in this country, as well as the world, has hopes and dreams and a life they have envisioned. When pushed off that path one is defensive and can become violent. While the neighbor may need our help, their insistence of need is a detour many refuse to follow.

Robert Kennedy believed in the same principles and mentions them in depth in the third quarter of his speech on violence. In order to appreciate the history that shares those sentiments, it is important to understand more of what Wiesel stated in 1999. Through his words, society can see the message of Robert Kennedy pushing into this generations fight against violence and indifference.

> Over there, behind the black gates of Auschwitz, the most tragic of all prisoners were the 'Muselmanner' as they were called. Wrapped in their torn blankets, they would sit or lie on the ground, staring vacantly into space, unaware of who or where they were, strangers to their surroundings. They no longer felt pain, hunger, thirst. They feared nothing. They felt nothing. They were dead and did not know it.[12]

This was a very chilling and moving part of Wiesel's speech. He discussed the past and reflects on Auschwitz and discussed those prisoners with the most tragic of fates. He discussed those prisoners that just lied on the ground and did nothing. They felt no pain. To feel nothing is to lack life and to lack life is the abandonment of humanity. Human beings took that away from those prisoners and their indifference to the suffering of those held captive was the absolute destruction of humanity. These prisoners had lost their sense of belonging and their sense of what it meant to live. They are a perfect example of how someone thrown into a pit of despair created by indifference is lost to society and in the end they are lost to themselves. Indifference creates hopelessness and those that perpetrate it are a villain of another sort. As Wiesel continued,

> Rooted in our tradition, some of us felt that to be abandoned by humanity then was not the ultimate. We felt that to be abandoned by God was worse than to be punished by Him. Better an unjust God than an indifferent one. For us to be ignored by God was a harsher punishment than to be a victim of His anger. Man can live far from God—not outside God. God is wherever we are. Even in suffering.[13]

Wiesel tried to come to a conclusion as to what role God played in those horrible years during the Holocaust. He discussed how he and others felt that God had abandoned them, which was worse than being punished by him. Wiesel tried to convey the ultimate meaning and understanding of what it meant to be indifferent. Here they truly believed that God was being indifferent, and in that same sense they would rather have had an unjust God than an indifferent one. With an unjust God they would have been allowed to feel and appreciate their pain, but indifference is neither painful nor comforting.

Without salvation or damnation, what can one determine from their position and the future of their cause? This is incredible coming from a man that had lived through the worst event in human history. Although at the same time it is not surprising. Wiesel was trying to convey that through this horrible event, God's influence was lost and in so saying, the true power of indifference is the ultimate abandonment of hope in humanity, oneself, and the desertion of God. Wiesel continued,

> In a way, to be indifferent to that suffering is what makes the human being inhuman. Indifference, after all, is more dangerous than anger and hatred. Anger can at times be creative. One writes a great poem, a great symphony, one does something special for the sake of humanity because one is angry at the injustice that one witnesses. But indifference is never creative. Even hatred at times may elicit a response. You fight it. You denounce it. You disarm it.[14]

Indifference makes a human shed his skin and become something grotesque and unnatural. This is dangerous, this is sad, and this is what has plagued mankind then and now.

Everyone does something everyday and what they did or do will create a response from someone, either good or bad. Indifference is when nothing happens. As Wiesel described, anger is creative because it can elicit someone to write a wonderful song or a poetic speech attacking those that angered them, thus becoming informative to others. In the final analysis, even hatred creates a response. If someone hurts you, you may hurt them back. Simply stated, if someone attacks you because of your race, sexual orientation, religion, or gender, your response may be to be saddened by the utterance of hatred or to be strong and move forward. Either way individuals respond to hatred, but never to indifference. Wiesel continued,

> Indifference is always the friend of the enemy, for it benefits the aggressor—never his victim, whose pain is magnified when he or she feels *forgotten*. The political prisoner in his cell, the hungry children, the homeless refugees—not to respond to their plight, not to relieve their solitude by offering them a spark of hope is to exile them from human memory. And in denying their humanity we betray our own. Indifference, then, is not only a sin, it is a punishment.[15]

The horrible truth for humanity is that indifference is the end, and the fact that humanity in many regards has witnessed this type of perversion is one of the saddest things to realize. When someone is hurt or becomes a victim from a senseless act of violence and is then forgotten, the pain they felt is, as Wiesel explains, heightened. This is the same for all victims of every type of crime. When a person refuses to help the homeless or feed a child they crush that person's spirit and destroy their surroundings. As Wiesel explains, societies have devastated their human sense and deceive our own. Through the indifference of all, the incredible story of all those left to wallow through inaction becomes untold and unnoticed. Their ambition falls into the abyss of human history and through that journey society destroys a piece of who they are. This is our fate if people refuse to move from the path which they have chosen to follow.

Too often people focus on their own lives and only pay attention to those that would upset and uniquely satisfy their everyday lives. Many see the world, but are lacking the ability to see the greater picture around them. These same people will go to the most beautiful cities in the world and marvel at the architecture of great buildings and listen to the majesty of wonderful music, but at the same time they walk by many that live in poverty and countless individuals whose future is unappreciated. Little by little, they become an imaginary blemish on society, pushed to the side and forgotten. For a final resting place, these individuals that live their lives in the shadow of splendor and triumph slowly create a world at odds with understanding and appreciation. Their story is our loss and our indifference is their world.

As Robert Kennedy stated in a lecture at the University of Johannesburg in South Africa in June of 1966,

> We all struggle to transcend the cruelties and the follies of mankind. That struggle will not be won by standing aloof and pointing a finger; it will be won by action, by men who commit their every resource of mind and body to the education and improvement and help of their fellow man.[16]

As stated earlier, many lessons can be learned from the spoken word. Society would be wise to learn from the wisdom of those that have witnessed or lived through violence and hatred. This is in order to create a better world for all. Elie Wiesel, speaking out about indifference, which will always be a friend of violence and an enemy of reason, spoke of the need to understand what it meant to be indifferent and the terrible effect that such a stance can elicit. As he stated, it is so easy to look away from the victims of violence and act with indifference, but in that end it only acts to cripple everyone involved. Of course it is easier to look away, simple not to care, and effortless to feel worse with inaction, but it is this lack of action that leads to the rise of hostility. Both Wiesel and Kennedy seemingly knew that the course of inaction, which had been created, was dangerous. As Dante once wrote and Kennedy liked to quote, "The hottest places in Hell are reserved for those who in time of moral crisis preserve their neutrality."[17] Then and now, the path that has for years been paved has begun to crack with the chill of indifference.

Robert Kennedy continued his speech and a great deal of it resembled the commentary of Wiesel. Kennedy said,

> *For there is another kind of violence, slower but just as deadly destructive as the shot or the bomb in the night. This is the violence of institutions; indifference and inaction and slow decay.*

In all reality, what Kennedy was announcing was along the same lines as what Elie Wiesel said in his speech on indifference. In the world, bombs can explode and kill innocent people, a gunman can kill innocent people, but at the same time that is not the only type of violence that can destroy. When people stop caring about one another as human beings and stop respecting people's rights as human beings, everyone becomes a victim to a new form of violence. Indifference, as Wiesel said, is more dangerous than anger, it is more sinister than hatred, and indifference is emotionless. As Wiesel expressed,

> I think the greatest source of danger in this world is indifference. I have always believed that the opposite of love is not hate, but indifference. The opposite of life is not death, but indifference. The opposite of peace is not war, but indifference to peace and indifference to war. The opposite of culture, the opposite of beauty, the opposite of generosity is indifference. Indifference is the enemy.[18]

As Wiesel sees it, indifference is the greatest threat to humanity and in that same sense a stimulant to violence. As Robert Kennedy expressed regarding change,

> A revolution is coming—a revolution which will be peaceful if we are wise enough; compassionate if we care enough; successful if we are fortunate

enough—but a revolution which is coming whether we will it or not. We can affect its character; we cannot alter its inevitability.[19]

The act of indifference is neither good nor bad, neither care nor fear, and for Wiesel and Kennedy this is the slow decay of society.

When people do not act to help others, do not provide a glimmer of caring, then society too becomes a victim of indifference. But this level of indifference is growing at a pace unmatched in history. With the growing access to new weaponry, and people being referred to as "physiologically broken," then there is no surprise that all of these school shootings and random shootings take place in our society. With indifference at such a high degree it is also interesting to note that people resort to violence for reasons like becoming famous. It is not even that they are angry, or even sad, they simply want to act out of circumstances that have nothing to do with the people they are hurting. These individuals are indifferent to the fact that they are hurting anyone. The shooters seem to look past that consequence and focus solely on their own glory or internal pain. This is what fuels violence and in that same regard what has decayed the structure of society.

When good people do nothing, society is left unprotected. Allowing evil and violence to continue and cloak it under the blanket of "human nature," is an act of indifference in its own right. As Robert Kennedy stated, "The innocent suffer—how can that be possible and God be just. All things are to be examined and called into question—There are no limits set to thought."[20] All individuals should look at their own lives and contributions. The other day I had a conversation with a colleague that opposed the new Massachusetts Health Care system that makes it mandatory to have health insurance. This colleague was angered by the fact that the government would demand everyone to have health insurance and did not like the fact that the government used taxes to fund the health coverage of those that do not make enough money to pay for it on their own. Although, I respected my colleague's opinion and ability to logically think about this political issue, I disagreed over who should fund the coverage. I told this colleague that the new law was a great step in the right direction. Finally people that could not afford health insurance could gain access to it. People that made too much money for free health insurance and could not afford private health insurance could have access to what should be considered such a basic need of life. He did not agree that a person should pay higher taxes to fund health insurance. I said that it is true, it would be great for the government to pay for it all up front, but either way our taxes would be raised in order to fund the policy.

I truly believe that Americans pay so much in taxes anyway, and then still need to pay for their own health coverage, that it would be the best for all for the government to universally fund it and charge higher taxes. Truthfully, I am willing to pay the extra percentage in taxes if it means that when I walk down the street and see a mother walking with her child that I know that child will grow up in world where she or he will not have to worry about their ability to see a doctor or if they are able to afford their health bills. People refuse to want to pay taxes because they do not feel that they should be using their hard earned money to fund health insurance for people they do not even know. That "everyone" is indifference. As citizens of America there is an obligation to one another. When one suffers, all of society suffers. Robert Kennedy attacked poverty when he spoke at the Citizens Union in New York, New York on December 14, 1967. He stated,

> Let [television] show the sound, the feel, the hopelessness, and what its like to think you'll never get out. Show a black teenager, told by some radio jingle to stay in school, looking at his older brother, who stayed in school, and who's out of a job . . . put a Candid Camera team in a ghetto school and watch what a rotten system of education it really is. Film a mother staying up all night to keep the rats from her baby . . . Then I'd ask people to watch it and experience what it means to live in the most affluent society in history—without hope.[21]

There is an obligation to protect everyone in this country. People in this nation either can not afford health care or have literally no access to it. Health is a basic necessity of life and must be protected, because anyone can grow ill or infirmed at any moment. Society needs to start putting other people first, even before themselves. As Kennedy and Wiesel had both warned society about in their speeches, Americans cannot quietly or slowly lead down the path of inaction or indifference.

One of Kennedy's favorite poets, Robert Frost wrote a poem about two roads diverged in the forest. Along comes a traveler that must choose between the roads to travel down. He could easily choose the path that has been traveled upon often. Or he can choose the harder path, the one that is overgrown and has been traveled only rarely if at all. That is a question that I pose to all of you. Choose the easy path with no change, or the harder path that makes one stronger and the world better? Neither path is technically wrong, but one will change your life, while the other leaves the world the same. Imagine a world if everyone chose the harder path. Robert Kennedy spoke of this same idea of change when he addressed those at the University of Witwatersrand, Johannesburg, South Africa on June 8, 1966. In his speech titled "Final Message to White South Africa," Kennedy stated,

> Our choice is not whether change will come, but whether we can guide that change in the service of our ideal and toward a social order shaped to the needs of all our people. In the long run we can master change not through force or fear,

but only through the free work of an understanding mind, through an openness to new knowledge and fresh outlooks which can only strengthen the most fragile and the most powerful of human gifts: the gift of reason.[22]

Robert Kennedy knew that change was inevitable in the United States and that society was capable of doing it with great wisdom.

While Robert Kennedy gave his speech in April of 1968, the country was a very different place than it is today. He continued,

This is the violence that afflicts the poor, that poisons relations between men because their skin has different colors. This is the slow destruction of a child by hunger, and schools without books and homes without heat in the winter.

The violence of inaction and the sadness of indifference are a type of sorrow that does not attack the upper-class or the well off, but rather as Kennedy says, "it afflicts the poor." I remember a trip I took to Texas in January of 2007 to visit a friend and celebrate his wedding. It was a great trip, and being in Texas I got to do something I never thought I would ever do and that was visit Dallas and see where President John F. Kennedy was assassinated. Of course it was extremely nice of my friend to take me to the area the day before his wedding, and it was an experience I will never forget. One interesting thing about a city like Dallas, Texas and really any city in America, is the number of homeless and poverty stricken individuals one comes across.

While walking around the city of Fort Worth, Texas on almost every corner I was met by an individual either asking for money or for a bus pass, and in one instance even being asked for just one piece of candy. It is extremely embarrassing and sad to say that at some instances I honestly did not have anything for the individual, and at other moments wanted to be left alone. Indifference affects the poor and poverty stricken more than most groups, because indifference by all will surely be their ultimate doom. I would love to have the ability to provide them with everything they need and do anything to help them get off the streets. I was overcome with sadness, hoping that someday they would find the opportunity to upwardly move themselves out of the situation that they now find themselves in. But, as an adjunct professor trying to maneuver myself into the political world there is really not much that I can offer, except to write about these instances and bring more awareness to their cause.

Robert Kennedy addressed the University of Norte Dame in South Bend, Indiana on April 4, 1968 with a speech titled, "Child Poverty and Hunger." During this speech Kennedy attacked poverty in America and demanded action rather than idleness. He stated,

Action in adequate measure can wait no longer. There are children in the United States of America with bloated bellies and sores of disease on their bodies. They have cuts and bruises that will not heal correctly in a timely fashion, and chronically runny noses. These are the children in the United States who eat so little that they fall asleep in school and do not learn. We must act, and we must act now.[23]

As John Adams once stated, "The poor man's conscience is clear; yet he is ashamed . . . He feels himself out of the sight of others, groping in the dark. Mankind takes no notice of him . . . To be wholly overlooked, and to know it, is intolerable."[24] The problems of the United States are not new, but in an age of technology and wealth, this type of issue should be addressed in greater awareness. Robert Kennedy was aware of the "Other America" that sat below the poverty line and needed help from those above them. Still today they need help, but many refuse to acknowledge their plea. Kennedy's "Mindless Menace of Violence" speech acknowledges their risk. If societies are judged on how they treat those that cannot help themselves, then America has a long road to repair the damage that inaction has caused.

Robert Kennedy witnessed the level of poverty while he was on the campaign trial in 1968 and observed it his entire life while traveling. Although, Robert Kennedy grew up in a very wealthy family, he did not have to be poor to want to provide for the underprivileged. I feel that Kennedy, having grown up in a wealthy situation, had the ability to help more than anyone else. He saw, through his background, how things can be taken for granted, and how people seemingly lack the simple ability to care for those lacking the same lifestyle. Through this knowledge, Kennedy had a gift to use his status as a tool in the fight against poverty. Lyndon B. Johnson had made marvelous strides in helping the poverty numbers in the United States, but his spending for many of those programs had ceased because of the Vietnam War. Kennedy knew that the violence that afflicted society would also poison culture as a whole. At this time the group that found themselves under the poverty line and unable to find economic as well as social upward mobility were minorities, especially black Americas.

The fact that a man that has a different color skin keeps him for accessing education should be unacceptable in any society. With the lack of education that same person cannot access higher paying jobs. Therefore, this person is left on the outside looking in. Because of the color of their skin they are not allowed to move up the social ladder and therefore are left as an outcast with no sense of self worth. This, Kennedy saw as wrong and inexcusable and a point he wanted to make understood in the "Mindless Menace of Violence" speech. A symbol of this type of violence is a child going hungry in the richest country in the world. Another example is a child that cannot read because they have no access to books because the school they attend is not receiving the same funding, because it has black students and not white. Furthermore, in the richest country in the world there is no excuse for allowing children to starve and its schools to go without books. There is no excuse for families to be cold during the winter because they cannot afford their heating bills. There is no excuse for fear of violence today in those same schools. This was extremely rampant, especially in the 1950s and 1960s, with black Americans and other minorities not being allowed access to the country's many opportunities. Through these failures, violence is allowed to breathe free, indifference is allowed to slowly grow, and society is stalled from further progress.

All the sorrow combined together, results in many individuals not being able to find their self worth and discover the possibility of their ambitions. As Kennedy continued,

> *This is the breaking of a man's spirit by denying him the chance to stand as a father and as a man among other men. And this too afflicts us all.*

If society denies an individual, a man or a woman, from living up to their true potential based on their social status, race, cultural background, sexual orientation, religion, and gender their spirit is broken. This is not an issue of the 1960s, it is an issue of all generations, past, present, and future. This is an issue that affects us all. Yet, even so on the flip side of this cultural coin, what if an individual "is" given the opportunity and allowed to stand as a father or mother or as a man among men? In that instance, they are able to discover their own ability. The world is allowed to witness their ambitious outlook on society. The ability to dream is not a white and rich attribute, the ability to get a good education is not only for the smart, the ability to get a good job is not only for the people with "connections," the ability to hold public office is not constitutionally specified for the elite, and the task of shaping the world for the better is not only for the leaders.

As Robert Kennedy stated in a speech titled, "Crime in America" given in Indianapolis, Indiana on April 26, 1968, he demanded that the fight to create a better America was crucial for the equality of all.

> Thus, the fight against crime is in the last analysis the same as the fight for equal opportunity, or the battle against hunger and deprivation, or the struggle to prevent the pollution of our air and water. It is the fight to preserve that quality of community which is at the root of our greatness; a fight to preserve confidence in ourselves and our fellow citizens; a battle for the quality of our lives.[25]

All have the ability to dream and all should not be denied the path to reach those dreams. Of course, the task is not easy, which is why many do not try. But for those that are willing to take the leap, the path must never be blocked by indifference. The blocking of anyone's dreams is the blocking of possibility. As Robert Kennedy perceived the world around him, he viewed a land of wondrous possibility and to stifle anyone's hopes was to cripple the nation for underutilizing the ambitions of its citizens.

Robert Kennedy seemingly knew that what he was saying would be examined by his generation and future generations. He stated,

> *I have not come here to propose a set of specific remedies nor is there a single set. For a broad and adequate outline we know what must be done.*

Kennedy wanted to make it clear that he did not, in the course of this speech, propose a set of ways to fix the problems that were inflicting pain on America and the rest of the world. He was not there to set up a single set of remedies on what to do against violence. Rather, Robert Kennedy spoke of the terrible curse of violence in order to bring further understanding of how much pain violence can cause when perpetrated in a free and righteous society. He arguably knew that there was no clear cut answer on how to curb the growing level of violence in the world. He also knew that to do nothing, most assuredly meant that nothing would change. Kennedy also believed that the answer to these problems lie in the hearts and minds of society itself. He believed that everyone had the knowledge to stop the violence, stop the indifference, and stop the inaction.

Society must look at fellow Americans as if they are their brother or sister. Instead of looking at Americans as if they are the enemy, look at them as a friend. That means not only Americans that fit the image of what one sees in a friend, but rather everyone; black and white, Muslim and Christian, gay and straight, religious and atheist. In the end, everyone is human and all are mortal. Therefore as Kennedy stated,

> *When you teach a man to hate and fear his brother, when you teach that he is a lesser man because of his color or his beliefs or the policies he pursues, when you teach that those who differ from you threaten your freedom or your job or your family, then you also learn to confront others not as fellow citizens but as enemies, to be met not with cooperation but with conquest; to be subjugated and mastered.*

As Kennedy declared, to teach a man to hate and fear his brother is to learn not to respect and love one another, instead they learn to confront each other as enemies. Kennedy preached of what could happen if things did not change. In many places in this world, children are taught to hate other groups of people because of their skin color, cultural or religious background. This of course is no different in America, especially in the 1960s.

In America, there was something known as the "Nativist Movement" whose task it was to stop immigration into the United States. They had been taught that those immigrants coming to the United States threatened their freedom. This was true during the Red Scare of the 1920s and 1950s, when the country feared a Communist take over. It was also true in instances where people feared that immigrants would take their jobs and therefore they would not be able to pay their bills. In that end, people feared that they would not be able to provide for their families and secure the opportunity for their children's future.

An example in American history of fear while feeling threatened occurred in the 1920s. The greatest instance of anti-immigrant hysteria that took place in America, during the 1920s, came in the form of a trial of two men in Massachusetts. Ferdinando Nicola Sacco and Bartolomeo Vanzetti were two Italian-born American laborers and anarchists, who were tried, convicted and executed by electrocution on August 23, 1927 in Massachusetts for the 1920 armed robbery and murder of two clerks. Many historians have concluded that the Sacco and Vanzetti prosecution, trial, and aftermath constituted a blatant disregard for political civil liberties. Many critics of the case also felt that the authorities and jurors were influenced by strong anti-Italian prejudice and a bias against immigrants widely held at the time, especially in New England.[26] This is of course just one example of how people had such great fear of anything different. Whether it was immigrants taking one's job or Communists taking one's freedom, to be taught this level of fear creates panic and creates a new level of violence that is difficult to contain.

When Kennedy discussed that if a person teaches a man that he is lesser by his beliefs or his polices that he pursues, Kennedy was directly attacking the racial prejudice rampant in the United States at that time. If a man grows up being told that he is inferior and because of his skin color will never attain the level of society that he wishes to, this not only makes that individual feel less of a man, but also that there can never be any level of cooperation between the two bodies. The end result of this type of confrontation is potential violence. In a speech to migrant workers in California and New York in 1966 and 1967 Kennedy stated, "If there is anything that we've learned during the 1960s, all of us who are here, it is that violence is not the answer to our problems." He continued,

And let no one say that violence is the courageous way, that violence is the short route, that violence is the easy route. Because violence will bring no answer: It will bring no answer to your union; it will bring no answer to your people; it will bring no answer to us here in the United States, as a people.[27]

As Kennedy stated a short route accompanied by violence will never be the correct answer in a just and moral society.

In the end as Kennedy continued in his "Mindless Menace of Violence" speech. He discussed,

We learn, at the last, to look at our brothers as aliens, men with whom we share a city, but not a community; men bound to us in common dwelling, but not in common effort.

When individuals in society are taught to fear one another they learn to separate as a society with no clear hope of being united. Kennedy used the term "alien" to describe how Americans will eventually look at each other. It is an interesting word choice, but one that strikes a very strong cord with anyone listening. Remember, at many times in American history, especially today there are negative feelings towards many immigrant groups, especially those that come to the United States illegally. Kennedy was saying that Americans will eventually become so distant from one another through fear that it will be as if no one shares any common traits. Each American lives in this country, in a state, in a town or a city, but the idea of the community and civility will be lost when people teach each other to fear those that are different. Kennedy goes further using the term "bound" in references to the fact that society is attached to the same dwelling, meaning the United States, but our goal and vision of the United States is not shared. Therefore the effort to create a better society will surely travel different paths. This must change.

It is imperative, as I believe Kennedy tried to convey, that members of society begin to respect one another for who and what they are. He continued with this point,

We learn to share only a common fear, only a common desire to retreat from each other, only a common impulse to meet disagreement with force. For all this, there are no final answers.

While the goals of this society continue to separate as time goes on and the bonds that have joined this nation continue to tear, society grows closer only in a common fear. Through fear our society is similar. Through fear our society is linked together. Through fear our society will begin to destruct. Through fear our society will begin to grow violent to a new degree. By definition fear is an emotional response to impending danger that is tied to anxiety. Through indifference and the missteps taken, fear is the emotional state that will eventually bind society together if violence is allowed to continue down the slippery slope which American society has placed it on and to which it is currently on. After September 11, 2001 and in an age of terrorism, Americans learn to fear those that seem different than the average norm. Many look at Muslims as terrorists, pro-choice advocates as baby killers, and yet these negative and fearful connotations are so off the mark that through their misstep society is degraded.

I know as well as anyone that as Kennedy ends, there are no final answers to the problems being brought up. No final answers. Then what does one do to move on in the wake of these possibilities? As has been said, Kennedy has not attempted to be the grand authority on how to fix the world, rather setting his image up as a moral authority with advice and information to help in shaping the nation's next step. If society does nothing, things will remain as they are, as Kennedy alludes to. By providing this analysis of violence, indifference, and commentary on society's missteps, he paved a path that only our society can walk on. He cannot do the work for us. He cannot walk the path for us. Each American must take the key and unlock the possibility that lie in hope. Being told of what is wrong must initiate the next phase of the journey. Either through the election of those individuals that agree with the need to change or by proposing new ways in bringing people together in common respect, rather than common fear.

When people learn to respect each other as neighbor, family, and friend they learn to open themselves up to the possibilities of togetherness. From that idea society may move forward. Although on separate paths at the moment, Americans may move toward a day when those paths might diverge and grow into one another, forming one path leading to the same common goal for all of American society. A common goal for all allows the country to live up to its potential and then proceed to spread its message to the rest of the world. Only when America is reunited under one goal and unified against indifference and violence, will our society be ready to practice what it has preached. This must be done not for ourselves but for everyone else. Whether it is for the past, the present or the future, move forward with Kennedy's words as a guide, not a solution, and from there join together as one. As Kennedy stated,

> To say that the future will be different from the present is, to scientists, hopelessly self-evident. I observe regretfully that in politics, however, it can be heresy. It can be denounced as radicalism or branded as supervision. There are people in every time and every land who want to stop history in its tracks. They fear the future, mistrust the present, and invoke the security of a comfortable past which, in fact, never existed.[28]

People must never fear what they do not know. The future is our canvas, and individuals may paint any picture they envision with any colors, any stroke, and any way they please. Let us do this in peace and in a common effort.

NOTES

1. Horowitz, *On the Edge,* 190, 198–201.

2. Winston Churchill, "I have Nothing to offer but Blood, Sweet and Tears," (Speech delivered in the House of Commons in London, England on 13 May 1940). Quoted in Simon Sebag Montefiore, *Speeches that Changed the World* (London: Smith Davies Publishing, 2005), 90–93.

3. Simon Sebag Montefiore, *Speeches that Changed the World* (London: Smith Davies Publishing, 2005), 215–216.

4. Montefiore, 215.

5. Montefiore, 215.

6. Montefiore, 215.

7. Bill Clinton, "You Have Taught us Never to Forget," (Introduction given at the Seventh White House Millennium Evening in Washington, D.C. on 12 April 1999). Transcripts of speech located in the Library of Congress in Washington, D.C.

8. Chafe, *The Unfinished Journey, 513.*

9. Elie Wiesel, "Perils of Indifference," (Speech on indifference delivered at the Seventh White House Millennium Evening in Washington, D.C. on 12 April 1999). Transcripts of speech located in the Library of Congress in Washington, D.C.

10. Wiesel, "Perils of Indifference," 12 April 1999.

11. Wiesel, "Perils of Indifference," 12 April 1999.

12. Wiesel, "Perils of Indifference," 12 April 1999.

13. Wiesel, "Perils of Indifference," 12 April 1999.

14. Wiesel, "Perils of Indifference," 12 April 1999.

15. Wiesel, "Perils of Indifference," 12 April 1999.

16. Robert Kennedy, "A Final Message to White South Africa," (Speech delivered at the University of Witwatersrand in Johannesburg, South Africa on 8 June 1966). Robert F. Kennedy Senate Files Archive in the John F. Kennedy Library, part of the National Archives.

17. Dante quoted by Robert Kennedy at Columbia and Bernard Democratic Club in New York, New York on 5 October 1964. Quoted in *Make Gentle the Life of This World: The Vision of Robert F. Kennedy*, written by Maxwell Taylor Kennedy. (New York: Broadway Books, 1998), 7.

18. Elie Wiesel, "The Opposite of Love is Not Hate, It's Indifference," (Wiesel quoted in *US News and World Report* on 27 October 1986). *US News and World Report.* (7 June 2008).

19. Robert Kennedy, "Regarding the United States Policy in Latin America," (Speech regarding change in society delivered in the United States Senate in Washington, D.C. on 9 and 10 May 1966). Robert F. Kennedy Senate Files Archive in the John F. Kennedy Library, part of the National Archives.

20. Arthur M. Schlesinger J. *Robert Kennedy and his Times* (New York: Mariner Books, 2002), 617.

21. Robert Kennedy, "A Holiday Reflection for White America," (Speech delivered at the Citizens Union in New York, New York on 14 December 1967). Robert F.

Kennedy Senate Files Archive in the John F. Kennedy Library, part of the National Archives.

22. Robert Kennedy, "A Final Message to White South Africa."

23. Robert Kennedy, "Child Poverty and Hunger," (Speech delivered at the University of Notre Dame in South Bend, Indiana on 4 April 1968). Robert F. Kennedy Senate Files Archive in the John F. Kennedy Library, part of the National Archives. Quoted in *Make Gentle the Life of This World: The Vision of Robert F. Kennedy*, written by Maxwell Taylor Kennedy. (New York: Broadway Books, 1998), 59.

24. Robert Kennedy, *To Seek a Newer World* (Boston: DoubleDay, 1975). John Adams, quoted by Robert F. Kennedy, 35.

25. Robert Kennedy, "Crime in America," (Speech delivered in Indianapolis, Indiana on 26 April 1968). Robert F. Kennedy Senate Files Archive in the John F. Kennedy Library, part of the National Archives.

26. Horowitz, 109.

27. Robert Kennedy, "Speech to Migrant Workers," (Speech delivered in Delano, California, and Monroe County, New York on March 1966, September 1967, and March 1968). Robert F. Kennedy Senate Files Archive in the John F. Kennedy Library, part of the National Archives. Quoted in *Make Gentle the Life of This World: The Vision of Robert F. Kennedy*, written by Maxwell Taylor Kennedy. (New York: Broadway Books, 1998), 131.

28. Robert Kennedy, "To Say that the Future . . . ," (Speech delivered at the California Institute of Technology in Pasadena, California on 8 June 1964). Robert F. Kennedy Senate Files Archive in the John F. Kennedy Library, part of the National Archives.

Chapter Five

The Same Short Moment of Life

I have cherished the ideal of a democratic and free society in which all persons give together in harmony with equal opportunities. It is an ideal which I hope to live for, and see realized. But my lord, if need be, it is an ideal for which I am prepared to die.

—Nelson Mandela

If any historical event can sum up the horrors of violence it is the American Civil War. For four years both North and South fought a bloody and gruesome war, not only to restore the union, but to set other men free. Over 620,000 Americans would die before the last bullet was fired. This type of bloodshed was the epitome, of what Robert Kennedy and many others, who came after Lincoln, warned about. Since the Civil War until the 1960s, a period of one hundred years, African Americans were denied their basic human rights. Kennedy lived at the end of that long and hard fought struggle for civil rights. While speaking in 1968 about violence, he knew all to well that America was as divided then as it had been just under a century before. America in the 1960s was a nation divided between those that opposed African American rights and those that supported it, those that spoke out against the Vietnam War and those that fought it.

When Abraham Lincoln was reelected president in 1864, he defeated George McClellan, who had once served as the General of the Army of the Potomac on two different occasions during the Civil War. When Lincoln gave his second and final Inaugural Address, he discussed what he felt was God's position towards his warring country. Lincoln addressed the crowd with a man by the name of John Wilkes Booth in attendance. He stated,

If we shall suppose that American slavery is one of those offenses which, in the providence of God, must needs come, but which, having continued through His appointed time, He now wills to remove, and that He gives to both North and South this terrible war as the woe due to those by whom the offense came, shall we discern therein any departure from those divine attributes which the believers in a living God always ascribe to Him? Fondly do we hope, fervently do we pray, that this mighty scourge of war may speedily pass away. Yet, if God wills that it continue until all the wealth piled by the bondsman's two hundred and fifty years of unrequited toil shall be sunk, and until every drop of blood drawn with the lash shall be paid by another drawn with the sword, as was said three thousand years ago, so still it must be said 'the judgments of the Lord are true and righteous altogether.'

With malice toward none, with charity for all, with firmness in the right as God gives us to see the right, let us strive on to finish the work we are in, to bind up the nation's wounds, to care for him who shall have borne the battle and for his widow and his orphan, to do all which may achieve and cherish a just and lasting peace among ourselves and with all nations.[1]

This speech indicated what Lincoln perceived as the reason behind the unspeakable savagery of the war. Lincoln had come to believe that the war was punishment from God for the sins of human slavery. With the war not yet over, he gave this terrible declaration. This was an incredible statement for a president to utter. As the war came to a close and the Union regained control over the country, Abraham Lincoln was assassinated by John Wilkes Booth on Good Friday, April 14, 1865. As Secretary of War Edwin M. Stanton would say, "He now belongs to the ages." Ironically, he died on the believed day that Jesus Christ died, thus propelling his image to Christ like status.

Lincoln would become one of the last victims of the violence that shook the country during the Civil War. In the end, the country moved on, in many instances in the wrong direction, especially in regards to civil rights for African Americans and former slaves. But it went in the right direction in regards to the rebuilding and restructuring of the government. Sadly, it would take some time for the country to completely reform and over a hundred years for African Americans to gain their civil rights. Still the United States, as Shelby Foote said became an "is" rather than an "are." Even William Faulkner said that history itself in its overall observance is not "was," but rather it "is."[2]

Historian Barbara Fields was once asked who won the Civil War. She answered, "the Civil War was a victory in the fact that the Union held their weapons at the end of the battles."[3] The soldiers who fought in the war, the generals who lead their troops into battle, the president who presided over the conflict, those are who won. Yet, if society diverges from the normal idea of just talking about the battles that ended with Appomattox, but instead focus on the struggle to make something better and higher out of the country, then the question becomes more complicated. Fields stated that slaves won the war and they lost the war.[4] They won freedom, that is the removal of slavery, yet they did not win their freedom, as they perceived freedom to be. Society must remember that as Faulkner once said history is, like the Civil War, an "is." The Civil War lives in the present as well as in the past. Fields argued that the generation that fought the war, the generation that had to pay the price in blood, the generation that had to pay the price in ruined futures, so established the standard that will remain until our society can finish the work.[5] Everyone in America can look and say that slavery no longer exists. People look at each other as citizens, regardless of race or background. So, then people have a task to do to "make sure that that too is not a joke." Fields commented, "If some citizens live in houses while others live on the streets, then the Civil War is still going on. The Civil War is still being fought" and unfortunately the Civil War as it is today can easily be lost and with it the hope that people desire to fulfill.[6]

As Barbara Fields understands and Kennedy discussed, the Civil War was over in one sense but still being waged in another. Americans must never forget the violence that occurred during the Civil War, and never forget the indifference that brought the war to fruition. As people must appreciate, and as Robert Kennedy and Elie Wiesel have pointed out, indifference and violence walk side by side into the tunnel of darkness. Slavery was an example of a deep rift that had occurred between people based on race. In the 1960s America still struggled with that issue of race, and our society does so today. Society heals constantly from this terrible blemish. Lincoln's victory was not only a victory to restore the union, but a victory to make sure that never again would America preserve the concepts of slavery into American law. Kennedy wanted to express what he felt needed to be done to erase those thoughts from the hearts and minds of men forever. He did so not only for his generation but for the future's attitudes towards race and difference.

Robert Kennedy was beginning to come to the close of his speech and, the ending of the speech offers a glimmer of hope for the future. While the previous portion of his speech dealt with the pains and troubles he felt were fracturing the country, he now offered an opinion of how things could change. Kennedy tried to paint a picture for his listeners and future readers of what could be done to curb the level of violence in America. He stated,

Yet we know what we must do. It is to achieve true justice among our fellow citizens. The question is not what programs we should seek to enact. The question

is whether we can find in our own midst and in our own hearts that leadership
of humane purpose that will recognize the terrible truths of our existence.

As Robert Kennedy moved towards the conclusion of his speech, he wanted
to illustrate the hope that could be used to answer the dismay he had brought
forth in word. He did so by stating that everyone in the audience, future generations, and anyone who would listen to his speech, knew what must be done
to curb the level of violence and began anew to create a more moral society.
Kennedy mentions the need to achieve "justice."

Before Socrates was executed for practicing philosophy, he engaged in a
very heated debate regarding the meaning of justice. In the *Republic*, Plato,
speaking through his teacher Socrates, sets out to answer two questions. What
is justice? Why should humans be just? While among a group of both friends
and enemies, Socrates poses the question, "What is justice?"[7] At one point,
"Cephalus, a rich, well-respected elder of the city, and host to the group, is
the first to offer a definition of justice."[8] Cephalus' definition of justice is that
justice means living up to your legal obligations and being honest. Although
surrounded in good qualities, Socrates easily defeated this argument with a
counter example that stated that, justice would be like returning a weapon to
a mad man. Socrates went on and argued that,

> You owe the madman his weapon in some sense if it belongs to him legally, and
> yet this would be an unjust act, since it would jeopardize the lives of others. So
> it cannot be the case that justice is nothing more than honoring legal obligations
> and being honest.[9]

At this point Polemarchusm, Cephalus' son, took over the argument for
him. He then laid out a new definition of justice, which argued that justice
means that one owes friends help, and enemies harm.[10] Socrates then takes on
several points of this argument. Socrates points out that the judgment con-
cerning friends and enemies is weak. This idea will lead people to harm the
good and help the bad. As Socrates continued, "we are not always friends
with the most virtuous people, nor are our enemies always the scum of society" and that using justice to harm people can become a slippery slope.[11] Then
after a long debate with Thrasymachus, Socrates launched into a complex
chain of reasoning that leads him to conclude that injustice cannot be a virtue
because it is contrary to wisdom, which is virtue. Socrates then concluded
that justice is an adherence to certain common rules and in order for society
to reach these goals, it must conform to these regulations.

Although philosophers and historians look back at this argument as a dead-
lock, the importance of the argument was the ground that Socrates shook for
calling old ways into question. Just because an idea has always been believed,

does not necessarily mean that it is right, and Socrates proved that fact. Because he called old ways and old laws into question, the leaders of Athens saw him as dangerous, as well as the idea of philosophy. He was executed for trying to bring about a new concept of justice. Although at his time, not perceived in any great acceptance, Socrates tried to prove that justice was something good and desirable. He believed and wanted everyone to accept that justice was more than a principle, rather it connected to objective standards of morality and that it is in our best interest to accept and adhere to it.

Robert Kennedy in 1968 asked for his fellow citizens to again search for a new interpretation of justice, one with a true meaning. Of course, the definition of justice is interpretative, but Kennedy, like Socrates, was asking for the people to recommit to raising questions and refuse to accept a system that was currently uncooperative to human reason. As Robert Kennedy stated,

> In a democratic society law is the form which free men give to justice. The glory of justice and the majesty of law are created not just by the Constitution—nor by the courts—nor by the officers of the law—nor by the lawyers—but by the men and women who constitute our society—who are the protectors of the law as they are themselves protected by the law.[12]

Kennedy observed a system that had so far misused the concept of righteousness in the realm of peace and freedom. He saw a system that had misused the definition of justice for an unjust war in Vietnam. Kennedy concluded that this damaged the integrity of humanity and betrayed those people in America that were not white or wealthy. It was time for America to remember its creed and remember the importance of true and uncorrupted justice. In a speech titled "The Value of Dissent," which Kennedy delivered at Vanderbilt University, he stated,

> So if we are uneasy about our country today, perhaps it is because we are truer to our principles than we realize, because we know that our happiness will come not from goods we have but from the good we do together...We say with Camus: 'I should like to be able to love my country and still love justice.'[13]

Kennedy knew that it would not take a program to recognize the flaws that society had created, but instead the formula for this ailment was the people themselves. It is crucial for people, and society as a whole, to recognize and accept that America went wrong at some point in its past. Now, Americans must work to fix the terrible pains which have been inflicted on them and those around them.

A society that looks at one group as inferior, or a country where the rich live extravagantly and many live on the streets, is an America that has forgotten its duty to the people. Thus it must be redirected back on course. The political process can only take the work so far. The people can, by themselves, change the route and direction of society's attitudes. When indifference is allowed to continue, it will breed the very violence that inflicts a need for justice. When righteousness no longer works in unity with reason, it is up to the people to move forward. To look at fellow Americans not as neighbors but as strangers is a perversion of this very message.

Now, individuals may look at textbooks in high schools and colleges all over the country and find a history of America that is glowing and uncompromising. In all reality, our nation, like every state in the world, has had rough times and instances that can be seen as rather troubling. Although our history is one of beauty and the emancipation of the human spirit through democracy and freedom, those freedoms have sometimes come at the expense of others. Robert Kennedy believed this and he spoke of this in April of 1968. Right in front of his eyes, while the ink on his paper was not yet dry and the body of Martin Luther King Jr. not yet buried, he spoke of how African Americans, minorities, lower social class citizens, and many others needed to be respected for the essence of their ambition. Racial tensions in the country had brought the nation to its very knees, being overcome with the worst "racial disturbances" since the Civil War.

In the 1960s, and in 1968, the country was in the very midst of various radical movements and the struggle for equality was still on going and gaining momentum. Robert Kennedy asked everyone to look inside themselves. Could they quietly live in a country divided down racial or economic lines? Could they allow justice to go unprotected and abridged? He wanted everyone to dig deep within their soul and find the valor and moral leadership to stand up and demand change. 1968 was an election year and Kennedy felt he could provide that change in guidance if he, like his brother, was able to take the reins of presidential influence. He asked everyone to realize that the country must change, or the level of indifference and violence would surely continue and the innocent would pay the greatest cost.

As Kennedy moved closer to the end of his speech, his words grew stronger and his hope greater. He stated,

> We must admit the vanity of our false distinctions among men and learn to find our own advancement in the search for the advancement of others. We must admit in ourselves that our own children's future cannot be built on the misfortunes of others.

Americans and other citizens of humanity must and cannot live their lives at the mercy of others. Our society must be furthered on the principles of right, rather than lead by the principles of wrong. Americans need to realize that civilization has succeeded on the backs of others. Societies have moved forward by keeping them down. Kennedy demanded that by treating others with harshness, or taking away from them the very life they dreamed to live, people lose a sense of self. People become overwhelmed with vanity, and this attitude keeps people from realizing that their lives have been heightened at the expense of others. Through one hundred years of Jim Crow laws in the American South, or survival of the fittest in the economic world, society has built its children's futures on the "misfortunes of others." This is not the America Kennedy wanted to live in and one that he declared would change if elected.

In 1968, Kennedy asked for this to end. He believed that no one had the right to build their children's future at the expense of others. Everyone's son or daughter has the same right to gain an education, get a job, eat at the same restaurant, vote at the same booth, and live the same ambitious lives as anyone else's child. Society must move forward concerned, not indifferent, of those around them and those hurt by our actions. Instead of advancing our own lives and our own superiority and wealth, society should instead think of the advancement of those that need the help the most. Through the search to help others people find that they, as well, have been advanced like never before. This may not be the advancement of wealth in the sense of dollars. Rather in wealth that is earned through the enhancement of the human spirit. There is arguably no better achievement in the history of human kind than the success of knowing that one has lived so that others could grow. If society can begin to move forward on that new endeavor, then there is the possibility for the survival of hope. In all great reality, the very victim of the argument of human nature is hope. Through hope and ambition human nature's design can be changed.

Robert Kennedy's vision slowly worked its way into full scope and realization. The world of racial tensions and a place where the poor remained poor, while the rich grew wealthier, was through Kennedy's words being given a new goal. As Kennedy continued,

> We must recognize that this short life can neither be ennobled or enriched by hatred or revenge.

Robert Kennedy began to recognize that if the course of human civilization could be changed then it must be allowed to do so with the principles of justice and morality. In no way can a society ever progress if it uses revenge or hatred to prove its point. Society cannot improve its character or moral standing in the world by acts of violence out of vengeance. It is difficult to prove an argument when the aggressor demands a statement at the end the barrel of a gun. How can society ever look in the mirror with hope, if people perpetrate the very acts they hope to stop? As society has learned in 2008, even when acts seem justified and the people feel compelled to obey, there can be no achievement when hope is lost.

Although I am not a country music fan, I am a fan of the Dixie Chicks. Although this may provide me with grumblings from many, I respect them and their views, especially in regards to the invasion of Iraq. In 2003, ten days before the invasion of Iraq, the lead singer of the Dixie Chicks, Natalie Maines, publicly criticized President George W. Bush for his actions in preparing the country for what she perceived as an unjust war. Not only did the country music world label the Dixie Chicks as traitors and refuse to play their music, but they also received constant death threats. Natalie Maines did nothing more than speak out, which she has a constitutional right to do. Many including this author felt the same way, yet our opinions were vilified because at that time President Bush had high approval ratings. In 2008, the War for Iraqi Freedom has been labeled a mistake, the mission still not close to being accomplished, the mission was never pure, and President Bush has an extremely low approval rating. Although the Dixie Chicks are still vilified by the country music world, in the end they were right. In 2007 they received five Grammy Awards, winning every category they were nominated for. That is what I consider historical irony.

In the United States of America citizens are protected by the First Amendment of the Constitution to speak their minds. If a citizen has a problem with how the government is operating, he or she may say so without fear of retaliation from the government. But, in our history there have been times when the government has used its power to take away some of the civil liberties that Americans have not only come to expect but demand. During the James Adams presidency he, as a Federalist, instituted what were known as the Alien and Sedition Acts. The intent of these laws was to curb both internal and foreign threats to the governing power. Many political opponents of the Federalists, like Vice-President Thomas Jefferson, objected to the policies as acts against the civil liberties of the people. Many, including journalists, found themselves thrown in jail for speaking out against the government. In the United States this is unacceptable and when Thomas Jefferson became president in 1800 he quickly had the laws abolished.[14] Woodrow Wilson tried the same thing with the Espionage Act of 1917 and Sedition Act of 1918. Wilson was so concerned with minimizing dissent in the United States during World War I that he had this act passed which forbade Americas from using "disloyal, profane, scurrilous, or abusive language" about the United States government, flag, or armed forces during the war.[15] When the Espionage Act made it a crime to help wartime enemies of the United States, the Sedition Act went after anyone that did anything or said anything against the government.[16] This is clearly denied in the United States Constitution, but was actually upheld in a United States Supreme Court decision discussing that a limitation on one's civil liberties is justified during wartime. Eugene V. Debs, a socialist, was sentenced to ten years in prison according to the act.[17] So acts against American's civil liberties have occurred and might occur again if the people do not ask questions and move aimlessly down the path away from justice.

Many today see the Uniting and Strengthening by Providing Tools Required to Intercept and Obstruct Terrorism Act of 2001, also known as the USA PATRIOT Act, as another example of the United States government abusing its power under the blanket of national security. The acts passed forty five days after the September 11th terrorist attacks was approved by both houses of Congress.[18] But lately has been criticized for infringing on the rights of Americans and weakening protections of civil liberties. Those that oppose the law are angered by the law's ability to indefinitely detain immigrants, use "sneak and peek" searches through which law enforcement agencies can search businesses or private homes without prior consent or knowledge of the owner or occupant. Critics have also been angered at the expansion of "National Security Letters," which allows the Federal Bureau of Investigation to search telephone, email, and financial records without a court order.[19] The acts have also expanded the access of agencies in searching your business and even library records. Since the passage of the act, critics have scored several successes with challenges brought before federal courts regarding portions of the act.[20] Through these challenges the courts have ruled that a number of the provisions were unconstitutional. Again, people must always question and not allow one's anger over acts of violence to allow their rights to be taken away out of fear.

Americans must not follow like lambs to the slaughter but rather ask questions, demand change and stand up against the unjust use of political will. Political will must be directed in other useful ways and the most important course is to challenge the issue of violence and indifference in society. Members of society must seek to neither conquer these issues nor use revenge to quench their thirst. Attacking those that have issues, and using wrong means to seek change, was exactly the way Kennedy preached was the erroneous way to help society. Everyone has only so much time to spend on this planet, as Kennedy referred to "short life" in this passage, and it is wise not to waste that time with thoughts of hate. Instead replace thoughts of hate with understanding and the ability to work out differences in another way. The fact that revenge and hatred will never solve problems shows the listener that only through compassion and leading through reason will the course to non-violence be waged. Society therefore must begin.

When Robert Kennedy spoke in Cleveland, he was determined to have his message heard loud and clear. As Kennedy stated,

> *Our lives on this planet are too short and the work to be done too great to let this spirit flourish any longer in our land. Of course we cannot vanquish it with a program, nor with a resolution.*

America in the twentieth century has been a nation full of hope and prosperity, yet there has been another America that has been shaded to the glory of democracy. It has also been a century of despair and a century of chaos. As Kennedy discussed our lives on this planet grow and fade in a blink of an eye. Still, it must be the goal of all to work to defeat the very violence and indifference that has violated the beauty of humanity. The work that was and is still needed, to create a better world for all, will not be easy to achieve and will not be finished over night. Yet the work must continue. As Robert Kennedy knew, future generations must take the baton and run with it and they too will need to pass it on to future generations to work on.

Robert Kennedy arguably felt that the struggle to destroy indifference and stop violence would not be completed while he was alive, and I know that the work may not be finished while I am alive. Yet, with this short time everyone must take the stick and run with it. People should not be afraid of what will happen if they fail. Americans should be excited at the possibility if they succeed. Nothing in life is accomplished with ease, and anything worth something will not be easy to obtain. Kennedy, again in this piece, believed that programs and resolutions will not end violence and indifference. The real success of this endeavor will come with a cleansing of the human spirit and a changing in the attitude of all mankind. Human beings must work together both, enemies and friends, black and white, rich and poor, all must band together and create a new world order. Only with a common effort and a common understanding will this endeavor gain momentum. This was the task of past generations. It must be the work of this generation. It will be vital to future generations.

As Kennedy moved towards the end of his speech on the menace of violence his message began to shift. His speech became an example of the possibilities that lie ahead for America and the world. Kennedy continued,

> *But we can perhaps remember, if only for a time, that those who live with us are our brothers, that they share with us the same short moment of life; that they seek, as do we, nothing but the chance to live out their lives in purpose and in happiness, winning what satisfaction and fulfillment they can.*

It is time that everyone realized that life is extremely short and that everyone will eventually die. It is a very difficult thing to realize, that someday you will not be around. What lies beyond life on Earth has been the question of the ages, but the unknown must not be cause to fear. What is done with that short amount of time is truly up to us. Everyone on this planet can either use their time respecting mankind or use it to spread a message of hate. To hate is clearly not the answer. Society must believe and accept that each one of us has a role to play in the bigger picture of humanity. Everyone in society must seek to live their lives as they wish to live them. Some want to be teachers, others doctors, others baseball players, some even congressmen, and anything that someone's heart might call on them to participate in. Everyone in the world has the right to dream and live the life that they imagined.

Happiness is not a privilege. It is a basic right of human and natural law. To take away someone's happiness for one's own personal satisfaction is a perversion of human will. The criminal and the law abider both take up the same amount of space on this planet. Both have the right to live their lives in happiness. To take away one person's right to live because of one's un-quenchable need to steal or the drunk driver that drives drunk only to kill an innocent family, is a denial of the right to be. No one should fear that they could be mugged and killed, or killed by a drunk driver. One is an act of vi-olence and the other an act of indifference created by the need to drink heav-ily and get behind the wheel of a car. Both of these incidents are examples of loss and a stealing from victims their right to live out their lives in pleasure and fulfillment.

Robert Kennedy took this one occasion to speak to the people about the fear that he had about the direction of society and the way human beings treated one another. Whether how blacks were being treated or the poor were being treated, or any victim was being treated, the result was more than could be accepted. Each person is another individual's brother and if society starts treating each other like family, then acts of indifference and violence will surely diminish. With this result, people can live out their lives with the am-bition and drive that cannot be taken away from them by those that oppose them. Instead, their possibilities become the wonders of society and through their work society will prosper. Americans should not wonder who will suf-fer next, but imagine who will succeed next. The dreams that become shat-tered become the tears of society and through death people learn to hate them-selves for the society that has been created. Inaction will allow for these terrible instances to continue and inaction is the crime everyone perpetrates. Everyone in society must look in a mirror and realize that the blame for soci-eties blemish is theirs to share.

The best part is that there is hope that this may not be the history that later historians write about. There is time to rewrite the story of the very age in which our society lives. Instead of looking at violence and indifference as in-curable and irreversible, people must change their thinking and instead at-tempt to alter the way they view others as well as themselves. The taking of the life of one is the loss of all. Americans turn on the television and watch the news of empty violence in America and around the world and then turn off the television in tears and agony. The television must remain on. People have an obligation to learn from the mistakes that our past has made. A day that the news tells of the drop in the level of violence should be worth the attempt to create change. This will not be easy, but the thought of helping those human beings that are loved and love, is worth the task and can surely change all. As Robert Kennedy concluded,

> *Surely, this bond of common faith, this bond of common goal, can begin to teach us something. Surely, we can learn, at least, to look at those around us as fellow men, and surely we can begin to work a little harder to bind up the wounds among us and to become in our own hearts brothers and countrymen once again.*

The Oklahoma City bombing, The Rodney King beating, Columbine shooting, the 1968 Democratic National Convention riots, assassinations, repression and abuse of black Americans in the South, Virginia Tech Massacre, and many more instances of violence and indifference are the types of crimes that stain the character of American society. The greatest problem is that these types of incidents continue to play out in everyday life.

When people begin to look at each other as friend instead of foe, they will begin to forge the bond of common goodness and from there wash away the sin of dismay. Becoming friends will teach our children to respect rather than react and to love rather than hate. There is no greater task in this world than to teach our children about the world that society desires to create. It must be the next generation that again finishes the journey. If society's children are taught to hate, then the work already done will have been in vain and the sufferings of the few will outlast and topple the hopes of the many. In retrospect, if Americans teach their children to love one another, then successfully the track will have been built and the journey begun. If those children are given the moral character from youth to counter oppression and violence, than in adulthood they can lead with the same traits. The Berlin Wall did not fall victim to weather, but rather the storm of change, hope and determination, which was used to stand up against injustice.

Our generation, as well as the next, must finally begin to look at others as fellow men and women, and forge that universal bond to become one. Whatever the issues of the past, whatever the problems one has with another, it is important and imperative to heal that wound not with aggression or vengeance but with hope and admiration. America must become a single country with a common goal, rather than individuals with singular understandings of our country. Hopefully soon the same energy that has separated many different types of people in this county will be used to bring people closer together. As Kennedy pointed out time and time again, and is important to the task at hand, this will not be an easy venture. But the hope of what could be diminishes the reality of what is now.

I think most people in society are tired of news reports of violence and the senseless bloodshed on American streets claiming innocent American lives. I am sure that if people could fix all the problems in this nation, they would. They do this so that they do not have to see a mother cry in agony over the fact that her infant son will not be around to reach adulthood because of a stray bullet from a nearby gang shooting. I am sure that most people would use their power to prevent a parent from feeling pure sorrow for the loss of their son who did nothing more than go to school and was shot. I am sure all of us would make sure that children went to school feeling safe, and husbands and wives went to work without fear of a terrorist attack, and that our children's children were able to live in a better world than the world our society currently lives in. Robert Kennedy above all had this hope and vision. His hope was that his children would live in the type of world that he discussed in April of 1968 in Cleveland, Ohio. Yet forty years later that incredible vision has gone unanswered and unaccepted. Millions of Americans go about their daily routines, unaware or unwilling to recognize the serious problems that affect not only society but their lives as well. Just because they may live outside the most dangerous cities in the country does not mean that they are fully safe from the menace of violence that inflicts fear in American society.

One cannot escape fear because as long as violence is allowed to move forward the fear within each and every single American will grow. As it gets bigger, so will the difficulty to destroy it. Many people are able to look the other way and feel, as discussed, the problems are too big. For many it is easier to forget about society's problems and go about their daily lives indifferent to the cries of others. If individuals in history had been indifferent to the cries of those being held victim to violence and suffering, then who knows how long the institution of slavery would have lasted or if it would have been abolished. How long would the world have waited to destroy Hitler's Nazi Germany and free the remaining Jews that Hitler had not yet killed because they were Jewish? Examples of suffering are endless, and at the same time so are example's of human righteousness. History is riddled with times that people stood up and said enough is enough. Men and women of all shapes and sizes and cultural and racial backgrounds have stood up and refused to be pushed back by the enormous wave of indifference. History shows us that people can make a difference, if even a small difference. Everyone must remember that in order to walk you must first take baby steps. Let this be our first step and from this society will surely run the marathon that finally brings down the level of violence. From action, courage, and concern will flow our journey to destroy violence and indifference and pave a new road towards harmony for future generations to appreciate.

In this journey, Robert Kennedy's vision will finally be complete. The most important thing to understand is that in order for his vision and message to succeed, it need not be finished, but only attempted. From the first attempt the work will move and the uncertain fate of this cause will surely begin. America today is ready for this message and willing to move towards this journey and moral endeavor. Remember, when the time comes for an individual to shuffle off this mortal soil, how will they want to be judged? When asked what one did with their life, will they be able to say that someone else's life is better because they lived? One need not become a hero, only subscribe to these old and new ideas and make the world a better place.

NOTES

1. Abraham Lincoln, "Second Inaugural Address," (Address delivered the United States Capital Building in Washington, D.C. on 4 March 1965). Original located in the Library of Congress in Washington, D.C.

2. "The Better Angles of Our Nature," *The Civil War*, prod. Ken Burns, 11 hours, PBS video, 1990, DVD.

3. "The Better Angles of Our Nature," *The Civil War*, prod. Ken Burns, 11 hours, PBS video, 1990, DVD.

4. "The Better Angles of Our Nature," *The Civil War*, prod. Ken Burns, 11 hours, PBS video, 1990, DVD.

5. "The Better Angles of Our Nature," *The Civil War*, prod. Ken Burns, 11 hours, PBS video, 1990, DVD.

6. "The Better Angles of Our Nature," *The Civil War*, prod. Ken Burns, 11 hours, PBS video, 1990, DVD.

7. Plato. *Five Great Dialogues*. Trans. by Benjamin Jowett. (Roslyn: Black, 1942).

8. Plato. *Five Great Dialogues*. Trans. by Benjamin Jowett. (Roslyn: Black, 1942).

9. Plato. *Five Great Dialogues*. Trans. by Benjamin Jowett. (Roslyn: Black, 1942).

10. Plato. *Five Great Dialogues*. Trans. by Benjamin Jowett. (Roslyn: Black, 1942).

11. Plato. *Five Great Dialogues*. Trans. by Benjamin Jowett. (Roslyn: Black, 1942).

12. Robert Kennedy, "In a Democratic society…" Quoted in *Make Gentle the Life of This World: The Vision of Robert F. Kennedy*, written by Maxwell Taylor Kennedy. (New York: Broadway Books, 1998), 105.

13. Robert Kennedy, "The Value of Dissent," (Speech delivered at Vanderbilt University in Nashville, Tennessee on 21 March 1968). Robert F. Kennedy Senate Files Archive in the John F. Kennedy Library, part of the National Archives.

14. "The Alien Act," July 6, 1798; Fifth Congress Enrolled Acts and Resolutions; General Records of the United States Government; Record Group 11; National Archives.

15. Horowitz, *On the Edge,* 101–102.
16. Horowitz, 101–102.
17. Horowitz, 101–102.
18. Brooker, *Public Opinion in the 21st Century*, 3–5.
19, Brooker, 3-5.
20. Brooker, 3-5 and 350–351.

Chapter Six

We Know What We Must Do

'Give me a place to stand,' said Archimedes, 'and I will move the world...'
Few will have the greatness to bend history, but each of us can work to
change a small portion of the events, and then the total—all of these acts—
will be written in the history of this generation.

—Robert Kennedy

What will the future be like if Americans do nothing to stop the level of violence from continuing down its path of destruction? Robert Kennedy, who
spoke out against the evils of violence and indifference asked for his fellow
Americans to work together to wash away this terrible mark on our society.
In the end, he was tragically destroyed by the same violence he sought to ex-
tinguish. Robert Kennedy's time on this planet was shorter than anyone could
have expected and anyone feared. The work he began must now be the work
our society continues. The best example of the opportunity that was missed
by Robert Kennedy's sudden and violent death came in the form of a eulogy
given by his brother Edward Kennedy. There are no better words to describe
the impact that Robert Kennedy had on this nation and those who loved him,
than with the following words. As Edward Kennedy said,

We loved him as a brother and father and son. From his parents, and from his
older brothers and sisters—Joe, Kathleen and Jack—he received inspiration
which he passed on to all of us. He gave us strength in time of trouble, wisdom
in time of uncertainty, and sharing in times of happiness. He was always by our
side. Love is not an easy feeling to put into words. Nor is loyalty, or trust or joy.
But he was all of these. He loved life completely and lived it intensely.[1]

The impression that Robert Kennedy's life had on his family is not that different than the influence his life has had on this nation and the entire world.

A life that he dedicated himself to with compassion is an example of how everyone should try and live their lives today. People, including myself, that did not meet Robert Kennedy or did not live when he lived, still feel sorrow that he was taken so soon. The feelings of what might have been, or what could have been, if he had not been the victim of indifference, still lingers in the hearts of our society forty years later. A loss of that magnitude should indicate that his living was important and what he had to say carried significance on the future course of human civilization. The influence of his life will be felt by generations to come.

As Edward Kennedy stated, Robert Kennedy was a man deeply motivated, trusted, and loyal and his life, though cut short, was not without completion. The fact that society still respects, admires, and trusts Robert Kennedy is an indication that people still need him and his message. As Edward Kennedy continued,

> A few years back, Robert Kennedy wrote some words about his own father and they expressed the way we in his family feel about him. He said of what his father meant to him: 'What it really all adds up to is love—not love as it is described with such facility in popular magazines, but the kind of love that is affection and respect, order, encouragement, and support. Our awareness of this was an incalculable source of strength, and because real love is something unselfish and involves sacrifice and giving, we could not help but profit from it. Beneath it all, he has tried to engender a social conscience. There were wrongs which needed attention. There were people who were poor and who needed help. And we have a responsibility to them and to this country. Through no virtues and accomplishments of our own, we have been fortunate enough to be born in the United States under the most comfortable conditions. We, therefore, have a responsibility to others who are less well off.' This is what Robert Kennedy was given.[2]

Robert Kennedy's ability to recognize the problems of society and attempt to correct those issues can be seen as an example of his moral character and vision for society. Although born fortunate, he took it upon himself to devote his life to public service. During the course of that service, Kennedy became devoted to those people that were less fortunate and needed help the most. His love for others was an unselfish characteristic and his understanding of sacrifice to help others, was what made Robert Kennedy an extraordinary human being.

All human beings have flaws in their human character and I am sure Robert Kennedy had flaws of judgment. Even so, he dedicated his life to bringing to others what many refused to even notice they needed. As Edward Kennedy continued,

> What he leaves us is what he said, what he did and what he stood for. A speech he made to the young people of South Africa on their Day of Affirmation in

1966 sums it up the best, and I would like to read it now. 'There is discrimination in this world and slavery and slaughter and starvation. Governments repress their people; and millions are trapped in poverty while the nation grows rich, and wealth is lavished on armaments everywhere.'[3]

Robert Kennedy recognized that the world was imperfect and that all over the world, people were starving, being oppressed, and through that idea he recognized that these are the works of men. These crimes are examples of our indifference to human beings around the globe. Even with the progress of peace comes the advancement of conflict. It is no surprise that in a world full of leaders, there are countries that repress their people in order to stop them from advancing in moral thought.

In 1989, the Chinese intellectuals, students, and labor activists banded together to publicly criticize the ruling Chinese Communist Party in the People's Republic of China. They vowed to fight for more basic freedoms, which they felt had been denied by their communist rulers. This incident became known historically as the Tiananmen Square Massacre where the military began a crackdown on protestors, which left a total of 200-3,000 dead, depending on the source of information.[4] As Andrew Nathan reported,

Following the violence, the government conducted widespread arrests to suppress protestors and their supporters, cracked down on other protests around China, banned the foreign press from the country and strictly controlled coverage of the events in the PRC press. Members of the Party who had publicly sympathized with the protesters were purged.[5]

Governments have and will continue to crackdown on opposition when those that ask questions stir the pot of discontent. I once heard in a movie, "the people should not be afraid of the government, the government should be afraid of the people." Governments function because of their people. The people do not function because of their government. Society must not allow for violence to be used by the government against its own citizens, but it occurs often.

This is the world I live in and the world Kennedy understood existed. Nations all over the world grow wealthy on the backs of their citizens. It is now the most important time in American history. It is time for this nation to not be part of the growing problem but rather become a part of the lasting solution. There is a need to have a country that works to improve itself, not through the sweat and tears of its men and women but, through their unique abilities. As a country united as one, people can explore the horizon of humanity and become a beacon to the rest of world. Not in aggression, as America has become during the Bush administration, but in tranquility.

People need to remember something else that Robert Kennedy expressed in his speech in South Africa. It was that slavery still exists today. When America fought the Civil War in hopes of eradicating the terror of slavery from this nation, it succeeded in the shadow of a blood stained flag. Over a hundred and forty years since the end of the American Civil War, there are many in the world that still find themselves classified as human slaves. Even though on September 25, 1926 slavery was abolished worldwide by the League of Nations in Geneva, Switzerland at the Slavery Convention, it still continues to thrive.[6] It is sponsored by some governments and is helped by the ignorance of the world. Experts today believe that there could be around ten to thirty million people held in slavery around the world. In 2008, slavery persisted as one of the most egregious human rights abuses in the world, which is rather incredible to imagine.[7] Today, slavery is the fastest growing criminal enterprise and the second largest illegal enterprise in the world, ranking behind the drug trafficking organization and tying the sales of illegal weapons.[8] Even the United States State Department estimates that between fifteen and twenty million individuals are trafficked into the United States to become slaves each year.[9] One of the most disgusting facts about slavery is that it is an extremely lucrative and profitable international business. Reports state that trafficking in the United States brings in just fewer than nine billion dollars each year.

America has made strides to eradicate this blemish on American and world society. President Bush in 2000 signed into the law The Victims of Trafficking and Violence Protection Act of 2000 (Public Law 106-386) which was passed to,

> Combat trafficking of persons, especially into the sex trade, slavery, and slavery-like conditions in the United States and countries around the world through prevention, through prosecution and enforcement against traffickers, and through protection and assistance of victims of trafficking.[10]

Before this law was enacted no comprehensive federal law existed to protect victims of trafficking or prosecute those that took part in this immoral business. Since this act was created and because of the fact that one year after its creation, the terrorist attacks on September 11, 2001 occurred, the countries mission was redirected and the course of this trade continues to grow. Since the act was passed, states like Connecticut have passed their own laws combating human trafficking, but still many Americans are unaware of this horrendous crime around them.

Of course the task of realization will not be a small leap. To combat this problem people must have political will and have a country united together with a moral determination to demand an end to these types of crimes. Edward Kennedy continued his eulogy with Robert Kennedy's own words,

> 'Freedom is not money, that I could enlarge mine by taking yours. Our liberty can grow only when the liberties of all our fellow men are secure; and he who

would enslave others ends only by chaining himself, for chains have two ends, and he who holds the chain is as securely bound as he whom it holds.'[11]

With this understanding of his brother, Edward Kennedy continued to discuss an America that his brother had died to protect. He discussed more of the issues that affected mankind. He continued,

'These are differing evils, but they are common works of man. They reflect the imperfection of human justice, the inadequacy of human compassion, our lack of sensibility toward the sufferings of our fellows.'[12]

Americans have, in a great sense, in the last few decades, become less compassionate and indifferent to the sufferings of those around them. When people look around and see that the most important thing to focus on is celebrities and whether or not they get a coffee or a tea, or whether they shave their head or not, or what store they shopped at, society again becomes enthralled in a culture of ignorance. People become glued to the news and television, waiting to find out who will get arrested next and who wore the worst outfit. This type of prioritizing of society's issues is a clear failure of our society in caring for one another. Most Americans do not look at celebrities that mess up and want to help them. Many people watch them to feel better about themselves and take the focus away from the real problems of the world. It is much easier to watch celebrities make fools of themselves than focus on the suffering in Darfur, or on the streets of American cites and towns. These are, as Kennedy expressed, the "common works of man," and this is especially true in our society.

America is an imperfect society in an imperfect world. For years this nation, as well as other nations, have been traveling down the wrong path regarding human compassion and this path will be difficult to redirect. But that does not mean that our society should not try. People need to stop thinking of themselves and the lives of the wealthy to diminish the pain of their everyday lives. Instead people should improve their lives by improving the lives of others. People should not focus on the things that matter not in society, but rather turn their attention to the things that carry substance. Remember that,

'Our answer is to rely on youth—not a time of life but a state of mind, a temper of the will, a quality of imagination, a predominance of courage over timidity, of the appetite for adventure over the love of ease. The cruelties and obstacles of this swiftly changing planet will not yield to obsolete dogmas and outworn slogans. They cannot be moved by those who cling to a present that is already dying, who prefer the illusion of security to the excitement and danger that comes with even the most peaceful progress. It is a revolutionary world we live in; and this generation at home and around the world, has had thrust upon it a greater burden of responsibility than any generation that has ever lived.'[13]

As Edward Kennedy discussed from Robert Kennedy's written words, Americans today cannot hold on to a present that is by definition already dying. Americans cannot continue to live in a world that society has grown apart from. This world can be a cruel and unjust place, and yet it can be a great and wonderful place. It is especially a place with very much promise. In that same respect, everyone must remember that this world is our home and it is the only one our people have.

In the movie *Inconvenient Truth*, an Academy Award winning documentary, former Vice-President, Nobel Peace Prize winner and author of *The Assault on Reason*, Al Gore asked the audience to look at a picture of Earth from outer space, and take their thumb and cover up the planet. While doing this, he asked everyone to remember that behind one's thumb was all of human history. Every single success and failure, tragedy and triumph, all that human beings know has taken place in that small object surrounded by an endless universe. Americans cannot allow the sadness around them to eclipse what America is meant to become. If violence and indifference are allowed to run rampant, then society will surrender. With their loss society will allow the destruction of the fundamental principles needed to secure a home for future generations. Today, society is encountering an environmental crisis, a problem with violence, and a difficulty coming to grips with the issue of indifference.

Today people drive cars that destroy the environment. These same cars are costing millions of Americans their paychecks to afford gas, which has become difficult to obtain from the Organization of the Petroleum Exporting Countries (OPEC), an organization made of twelve oil producing nations. In the last decade, Americans have witnessed the cost of oil go from an estimated twenty-eight dollars a barrel in the year 2000 to one hundred-thirty dollars in 2008. America is in the midst of a crisis, and yet our recent governing power refuses to focus on science and the ability to find new fuel sources. People live in a world that can send a man to the moon, but cannot find another efficient source of energy to power a car from one place to another. Society must rediscover its moral determination. It must work inside the public political arena, rather than the private sector, to find new sources of energy and save our planet.

Americans cannot keep saying how things will eventually change and how someday things will improve. These are the "obsolete dogmas and outworn slogans" that Kennedy warned needed to end. In 1968, Kennedy's generation had the enormous task of taking care of some of the most important issues affecting mankind. Americans today, forty years later, have had "thrust upon us the same type of burden of responsibility" that they did then. It is now our time to continue the work they began. Society must also realize that they did not fail in their endeavor. The ultimate battle that those in 1968 began is still being waged. Americans may live in a world filled with the illusion of peace, but they must realize that the mirage around them is a fantasy. Once that is accepted the healing can begin and the world can be changed.

The most crucial thing to understand is that every single person has it, within themselves, to change the world. As Edward Kennedy said in his eulogy of Robert Kennedy,

> 'Some believe there is nothing one man or one woman can do against the enormous array of the world's ills. Yet many of the world's great movements, of thought and action, have flowed from the work of a single man. A young monk began the Protestant reformation, a young general extended an empire from Macedonia to the borders of the Earth, and a young woman reclaimed the territory of France. It was a young Italian explorer who discovered the New World, and the thirty two year old Thomas Jefferson who proclaimed that all men are created equal. These men moved the world, and so can we all.'[14]

Edward Kennedy utilized the images of Thomas Jefferson, Martin Luther, Columbus, Joan of Arc and others to show that history and society can be changed from the ambitions and hopes of one person. They moved forward to create a new society. If one person in the past had the capability to do so, then all can move forward one by one. Many people believe that one person can do nothing against the problems of the world. Yet as civilization has seen there are examples of one man being able to create unfathomable tyranny. Therefore if one man can create terror, it should be understood that one man can help stop it. But, in the end it is the will of the people that needs to be understood in order to make this fact so. Edward Kennedy continued,

> 'Few are willing to brave the disapproval of their fellows, the censure of their colleagues, the wrath of their society. Moral courage is a rarer commodity than bravery in battle or great intelligence. Yet it is the one essential, vital quality for those who seek to change a world that yields most painfully to change. And I believe that in this generation those with the courage to enter the moral conflict will find themselves with companions in every corner of the globe.'[15]

The world that people live in today refuses to change with the tide of history. Many in 1968 recognized the political burdens that affected their society and accepted the responsibility to change the world for the better. Yet, today when it comes to some of the most important issue for mankind, the world refuses to accept the need of improvement. Americans need to respect that they are not alone in the world, in their ambition to create a new vision of hope in civilization. This society must begin the "moral conflict" and once that battle has begun, allies will come from all corners of the Earth to join in this monumental struggle. Realize that through war bravery is recognized by the many, but through compassion and moral courage the world can be changed by the few.

Edward Kennedy reiterated Robert Kennedy's hopes and dreams for society and allowed him to speak for himself through his written work. Kennedy stated,

'For the fortunate among us, there is the temptation to follow the easy and familiar paths of personal ambition and financial success so grandly spread before those who enjoy the privilege of education. But that is not the road history has marked out for us. Like it or not, we live in times of danger and uncertainty. But they are also more open to the creative energy of men than any other time in history. All of us will ultimately be judged and as the years pass we will surely judge ourselves, on the effort we have contributed to building a new world society and the extent to which our ideals and goals have shaped that effort.'[16]

I am sure that people are aware that the path that has been built for our society will not be easy to travel down. In that same end, it is easy to imagine that most will rather focus on "personal ambition and financial success" instead of giving all they can for the hope of all.

As Robert Kennedy stated and it is true in our society, the road that history has paved for us, as it did then, is the same and it requires sacrifice and the unknown. The generation that he spoke of began the journey and our society must follow on the same course. In the end, our goals, ambitions, and work to rebuild society will be judged by history, by those around us, and lastly Americans themselves must judge their own work. Kennedy believed that,

'The future does not belong to those who are content with today, apathetic toward common problems and their fellow man alike, timid and fearful in the face of new ideas and bold projects. Rather it will belong to those who can blend vision, reason and courage in a personal commitment to the ideals and great enterprises of American society.'[17]

Today there is the need for visionaries and those with the common sense to continue the work that Kennedy started. There is a great need for commitment, courage and above all the want to change society for all human beings not just for some. In the end, the future is our goal, and in that goal, the course of humankind in the midst of hostility and coldness.

It is very sad to think that some people will live their lives careless of the problems that are gripping not only America but the rest of the world. I fear the indifference that society has become riddled with and fear where empathy has hidden. While I fear that some people have turned their back on others in this world, I know that there are many that currently move forward with a vision of the future that glows with promise. Edward Kennedy continued,

'We then continue. Our future may lie beyond our vision, but it is not completely beyond our control. It is the shaping impulse of America that neither fate nor nature nor the irresistible tides of history, but the work of our own hands, matched to reason and principle that will determine our destiny. There is pride in that, even arrogance, but there is also experience and truth. In any event, it is the only way we can live.'[18]

Although the road ahead is long and winding, it must not be thought of as inaccessible. Rather America must move toward the goal with open eyes and open hearts and the basic understanding that although they may not see the end result of their actions, the path must be paved and the hope must be strong.

While Robert Kennedy's speech in South Africa was used by Edward Kennedy to eulogize him, the hope for the future speaks louder. The tide of history cannot stop the current of ambition. Our own hostility towards change can crush the route of our venture. Respect this prideful dialogue, because in all reality society cannot stand to think of the alternative. In the end, as Edward Kennedy said of his lost brother,

> This is the way he lived. My brother need not be idealized, or enlarged in death beyond what he was in life, to be remembered simply as a good and decent man, who saw wrong and tried to right it, saw suffering and tried to heal it, saw war and tried to stop it. Those of us who loved him and who take him to his rest today, pray that what he was to us and what he wished for others will some day come to pass for all the world.[19]

In the final analysis, Edward Kennedy asked that Robert Kennedy not be "idealized or enlarged in death beyond what he was in life." Instead he wanted his brother to be thought of as just a normal man. Like anyone in this world, Kennedy must be remembered as someone that saw what was wrong with several aspects of society and attempted with his own ambition to change the course of those problems. His attempts at changing society are an example of what our society, and future societies must also do. If one individual can make one person want to help those that suffer, then think of the possibilities if a million people inspire one person each.

Society must not fear what the future has in store for them, but rather work to create a future that everyone needs. The day that I drive down the street and do not encounter an incident of suffering, or think when driving home of those that do not have what their peers refuse to give them, will be a day that I may rest easy. It will be a day that I realize that the "Mindless Menace of Violence," which Kennedy demanded everyone appreciate and work to destroy, will forever be an aspect of history. If Robert Kennedy can inspire one man forty years after he died, then think of the amount of people our society can inspire forty years from now with our vision. In closing,

> As he said many times, in many parts of this nation, to those he touched and who sought to touch him. Some men see things as they are and say why. I dream things that never were and say why not.[20]

The last line of Edward Kennedy's eulogy is one that must not be forgotten. Robert Kennedy was the type of person that would walk down the street, or go to the poor areas of the country and see things as they were and demand change. He dreamed of things that were not in place and asked why they were not there. Instead of looking at things and asking why he asked why not. A man devoted to change and hope, Robert Kennedy's vision and words are forever important to our national image and spirit.

Today, America is in need of more inspirational figures, such as Robert Kennedy. Society requires those people that stand up against the enormous issues the world has bestowed upon them, but people need never look far. Read their speeches and remember what came before and what can come after. It is time for our generation and future generations to take the world by storm and work to show what the human capability can really achieve. Do you want to look back on Robert F. Kennedy's speech on the "Mindless Menace of Violence," and think of what could have been? With the tools of technology and the wonders of compassion, Americans and the world can finally strive to change and actually achieve this task. It is time to do as Kennedy asked.

NOTES

1. Senator Edward M. Kennedy, "Tribute to Senator Robert F. Kennedy," (Eulogy delivered at St. Patrick's Cathedral in New York City on 8 June 1968). John F. Kennedy Library, Boston, MA, part of the National Archives.

2. Kennedy, "Tribute to Senator Robert F. Kennedy," 8 June 1968.

3. Kennedy, "Tribute to Senator Robert F. Kennedy," 8 June 1968.

4. Andrew J. Nathan, "The Tiananmen Papers," *Foreign Affairs*, (January/February 2001).

5. Andrew J. Nathan, "The Tiananmen Papers," *Foreign Affairs*, (January/February 2001).

6. *National Underground Railroad Freedom Center*, 2008, <www.freedomcenter.org /slavery-today/> (May 2008).

7. *National Underground Railroad Freedom Center*, 2008, <www.freedomcenter.org/ slavery-today/> (May 2008).

8. *National Underground Railroad Freedom Center*, 2008, <www.freedomcenter.org/ slavery-today/> (May 2008).

9. *National Underground Railroad Freedom Center*, 2008, <www.freedomcenter.org/ slavery-today/> (May 2008).

10. 106th Congress, "The Victims of Trafficking and Violence Protection Act of 2000 (Public Law 106-386)," Public Law, 28 October 2000, www.state.gov/documents/ organization/10492.pdf, (28 October 2000).

11. Robert Kennedy, "A Final Message to White South Africa," (Speech delivered at the University of Witwatersrand in Johannesburg, South Africa on 8 June 1966).

Robert F. Kennedy Senate Files Archive in the John F. Kennedy Library, part of the National Archives.

12. Kennedy, "Tribute to Senator Robert F. Kennedy," 8 June 1968.

13. Kennedy, "Tribute to Senator Robert F. Kennedy," 8 June 1968.

14. Senator Edward M. Kennedy, "Tribute to Senator Robert F. Kennedy." Robert Kennedy, quoted by Edward Kennedy from Robert Kennedy's "Day of Affirmation" speech given on 6 June 1966. All found at the John F. Kennedy Library, Boston, MA, part of the National Archives.

15. Kennedy, "Tribute to Senator Robert F. Kennedy," 8 June 1968.

16. Kennedy, "Tribute to Senator Robert F. Kennedy," 8 June 1968.

17. Kennedy, "Tribute to Senator Robert F. Kennedy," 8 June 1968.

18. Kennedy, "Tribute to Senator Robert F. Kennedy," 8 June 1968.

19. Kennedy, "Tribute to Senator Robert F. Kennedy," 8 June 1968.

20. Kennedy, "Tribute to Senator Robert F. Kennedy," 8 June 1968.

Bibliography

To be ignorant of the past is to remain as a child.

—Cicero

JOURNAL AND NEWSPAPER ARTICLES

Associated Press. "3 Teens Indicted in Rape of Mother, Son." *MSNBC.com.* 19 July 2007. <www.msnbc.msn.com/id/19852756/> (2 September 2007).

———. "Boys Ages 8 and 9 Charged with Rape." *FoxNews.com.* 19 November 2007. <www.foxnews.com/story/0,2933,312146,00.html> (2 February 2008).

———. "Can a Video Game Lead to Murder?" *CBS News.com.* 6 March 2005. <www.cbsnews.com/stories/2005/03/04/60minutes/main678261.shtml> (7 June 2007).

———. "Man Opens Fire in Omaha Mall, Killing 8 before Committing Suicide." *USA Today.com.* 15 December 2007. <www.kval.com/ news/national/12170681.html> (20 December 2008).

———. "Police: 10 month old Pittsburg baby dies after rape, assault." *Associated Press,* 11 November 2007. <www.wpxi.com/news/ 14636292/detail.html?rss= burg&psp=news> (18 January 2008).

———. "Suspect Charged in Philadelphia Cop Killing." *CNN.com.*4 May 2008. <www.cnn.com/2008/CRIME/05/04/officer.shot. philadelphia.ap/index.html> (18 May 2008).

Cathcart, Rebecca. "Boy's Killing, Labeled a Hate Crime, Stuns Town." *New York Times.com.* 23 February 2008. <www.nytimes.com/2008/02/23/ us/23oxnard.html> (22 March 2008).

Chernoff, Allan and Brian Vitagliano. "Philadelphia Mom Bought Guns for Boy." *CNN.com.* 12 October 2007. <www.cnn.com/2007/US/10/12/ student.arsenal/index .html> (15 October 2008).

117

"Children and TV Violence," *American Academy of Child & Adolescent Psychiatry*. *AA-CAP.com*. Number 13, November 2002. <www.aacap.org/ cs/root/facts_for_families/ children _and_tv_violence> (5 June 2007).

Clarke, Thurston "The Heartbreak Campaign," *Vanity Fair*, June 2008.

Dill, Karen E. "Violent Video Games Can Increase Aggression." *Journal of Personality and Social Psychology*. *APA.com*. 23 April 2000. <www.apa.org/releases/ videogames.html> (5 June 2007).

Flock, Jeff. "5 Dead, 11 Wounded in Arkansas School Shooting." *CNN.com*. 24 March 1998. <www.cnn.com/US/9803/24/school.shooting.folo/> (9 April 2008).

Goldman, Russell and Richard Esposito. "Illinois Shooter Planned Campus Shooting for at Least a Week." *ABC News.com*. 15 February 2008. <www.abcnews.go.com/ US/story?id=429308> (24 March 2008).

Grossman, Lev. "Why the 9/11 Conspiracy Theories won't go Away." *Time.com*. 3 September 2006. <www.time.com/time/magazine/ article/0,9171,1531304,00.html> (12 October 2007).

Johnson, Kevin. "Police Brutality Cases on Rise since 9/11." *USA Today.com*. 18 December 2007. <www.usatoday.com/news/nation/2007-12-17-Copmisconduct_N .html> (23 January 2008).

Kalning, Kristen. "Does Game Violence Make Teen Aggressive?" *MSNBC.Com*. 8 December 2006. <http://www.msnbc.msn.com/id/16099971/> (4 May 2007).

Kocieniewski, David, and Gary Gately. "Man Shoots 11, Killing 4 Girls, in Amish School." *International Herald Tribune.com*. 3 October 2006. <www.iht.com/articles/ 2006/10/03/america/web.1003slay.php> (28 March 2008).

Nathan, Andrew J. "The Tiananmen Papers." *Foreign Affairs*, (January/February 2001).

Rao, Mythili. "Mayor: Officers in Taped Beating will be Fired." *CNN.com*. 19 May 2008. <www.cnn.com/2008/CRIME/05/19/police.beating/index.html> (19 May 2008).

Sniffen, Michael J. "Hate Crimes Rose 8 Percent in 2006." *Washingtonpost.com*. 19 November 2007. <www.washingtonpost.com/wp-dyn/content/ article/2007/11/19/ AR2007111900607.html> (8 February 2008).

Thompson, Linda. "Police Identify Gunman as 18-yrear-old Bosnian." *Desert News.com*. 16 February 2007. <www.deseretnews.com/dn/view/0,1249,660195221, 00.html> (17 February 2008).

Wiesel, Elie. "The Opposite of Love is Not Hate, It's Indifference." *US News and World Report*, 27 October 1986

SECONDARY BOOK SOURCES

Anderson, Terry H. *The Sixties*. Boston: Pearson Longman, 2007.

Belmonte, Kevin. *William Wilberforce: A Hero for Humanity*. Michigan: Zondervan, 2007.

Brooker, Russell and Todd Schaefer, *Public Opinion in the 21st Century: Let the People Speak?* Boston: Houghton Mifflin Company, 2006.

Chafe, Williams H. *The Unfinished Journey: America Since World War II.* New York: Oxford University Press, 2003.

Clarke, Thurston. *The Last Campaign: Robert F. Kennedy and 82 Days that Inspired America.* New York: Henry Holt and Company, 2008.

Edelman, Peter. *Searching for America's Heart: RFK and the Renewal of Hope.* Boston: Houghton Mifflin, 2001.

Horowitz, David A. *On the Edge: The United States in the Twentieth Century.* United States: Thomson Wadsworth, 2005.

Kennedy, Maxwell Taylor. *Make Gentle the Life of This World: The Vision of Robert F. Kennedy.* New York: Broadway Books, 1998.

Kennedy, Robert F. *To Seek a Newer World.* Boston: DoubleDay, 1975.

Klinkner, Philip A. *The Unsteady March: The Rise and Decline of Racial Equality in America.* Chicago: The University of Chicago Press, 1999.

Lawrence, Thomas. *Seven Pillars of Wisdom.* New York: Wordsworth Editions Limited, 1997.

MacAfee, Norman. *The Gospel According to RFK: Why It Matters Now.* New York: Westview Press, 2004.

Mckinley, James. *Assassinations in America.* New York: Harper and Row, 1977.

McPherson, James M. *Battle Cry of Freedom: The Civil War Era.* New York: Ballantine Books, 1988.

Montefiore, Simon Sebad. *Speeches that Changed the World.* London: Smith Davies Publishing, 2005.

O'Connor, Karen and Larry J. Sabato, *Essential of American Government: Continuity and Change.* Boston: Pearson Longman, 2008.

Plato. *Five Great Dialogues.* Trans. by Benjamin Jowett. Roslyn: Black, 1942.

Remini, Robert V. *The Life of Andrew Jackson.* New York: Perennial Classics, 1988.

Rosenberg, Norman L. *In Our Times: America since World War II.* New Jersey: Prentice Hall, 2003.

Salinger, Pater and Edwin Guthman. *"An Honorable Profession" A Tribute to Robert Kennedy.* New York: Doubleday, 1968.

Schlesinger Jr., Arthur M. *Robert Kennedy and his Times.* New York: Mariner Books, 2002.

Wood, Gordon S. *The Americanization of Benjamin Franklin.* New York: The Penguin Press HC, 2004.

SPEECHES AND PRIMARY SOURCES

Clinton, Bill. "You Have Taught us Never to Forget." Introduction given at the Seventh White House Millennium Evening in Washington, D.C. on 12 April 1999. Transcripts of speech located in the Library of Congress in Washington, D.C.

Henry, Patrick. "Give Me Liberty or Give Me Death" Speech delivered in the St. Johns Church in Richmond, Virginia on 23 March 1775.

Transcript located at the Patrick Henry Committee Center, St. John's Church in Richmond, Virginia.

Kennedy, John F. "Special Message to the Congress on Civil Rights and Job Opportunities." Televised address to the American people from oval office in the White House in Washington, D.C. on 19 June 1963. Public Papers, John F. Kennedy Library, Boston, MA. 483.

Kennedy, Robert F. "A Final Message to White South Africa." Speech delivered at the University of Witwatersrand in Johannesburg, South Africa on 8 June 1966. Robert F. Kennedy Senate Files Archive in the John F. Kennedy Library, part of the National Archives.

———. "Child Poverty and Hunger." Speech delivered at the University of Notre Dame in South Bend, Indiana on 4 April 1968.
Robert F. Kennedy Senate Files Archive in the John F. Kennedy Library, part of the National Archives.

———. "Crime in America." Speech delivered in Indianapolis, Indiana on 26 April 1968). Robert F. Kennedy Senate Files Archive in the John F. Kennedy Library, part of the National Archives.

———. "From You." Speech delivered at the Indiana University Medical School on 26 April 1968. Robert F. Kennedy Senate Files Archive in the John F. Kennedy Library, part of the National Archives.

———. "On the Death of Reverend Dr. Martin Luther King Jr." Speech delivered regarding Death of Dr. Martin Luther King Jr. from Indianapolis, Indiana on 4 April 1968. Robert F. Kennedy Senate Files Archive in the John F. Kennedy Library, part of the National Archives.

———. "Regarding the United States Policy in Latin America." Speech regarding change in society delivered in the United States Senate in Washington, D.C. on 9 and 10 May 1966. Robert F. Kennedy Senate Files Archive in the John F. Kennedy Library, part of the National Archives.

———. "Speech to Migrant Workers." Speech delivered in Delano, California, and Monroe County, New York on March 1966, September 1967, and March 1968. Robert F. Kennedy Senate Files Archive in the John F. Kennedy Library, part of the National Archives.

———. "The Color of an Executioner's Robe Matters Little." Anti-war speech given at the University of California, Berkeley on 22 October 1966. Robert F. Kennedy Senate Files Archive in the John F. Kennedy Library, part of the National Archives.

———. "The Value of Dissent." Speech delivered at Vanderbilt University in Nashville, Tennessee on 21 March 1968. Robert F. Kennedy Senate Files Archive in the John F. Kennedy Library, part of the National Archives.

———. "To Say that the Future..." Speech delivered at the California Institute of Technology in Pasadena, California on 8 June 1964. Robert F. Kennedy Senate Files Archive in the John F. Kennedy Library, part of the National Archives.

Kennedy, Senator Edward M. "Tribute to Senator Robert F. Kennedy." Eulogy delivered at St. Patrick's Cathedral in New York City on 8 June 1968. John F. Kennedy Library, Boston, MA, part of the National Archives.

King Jr., Martin Luther, "Mountaintop Speech." Sermon delivered at the Mason Temple (Church of God in Christ, World Headquarters) in Memphis, Tennessee on 3 April 1968. One night before Dr. King was assassinated. Manuscript is located at the Estate of Dr. Martin Luther King Jr. in Atlanta, Gerogia.

Letter from Abraham Lincoln to James C. Conkling, 26 August 1863. Original located in the National Archives in Washington, D.C.

Lincoln, Abraham. "Second Inaugural Address." Address delivered the United States Capital Building in Washington, D.C. on 4 March 1965). Original located in the Library of Congress in Washington, D.C.

O'Hurley, John. "2006 Providence College Commencement Address." Address given at the Dunkin Donuts Center in Providence, Rhode Island on 21 May 2006. Transcript located at Providence College, Providence, Rhode Island.

Wiesel, Elie. "Perils of Indifference." Speech on indifference delivered at the Seventh White House Millennium Evening in Washington, D.C. on 12 April 1999. Transcripts of speech located in the Library of Congress in Washington, D.C.

TELEVISION SOURCES

Amazing Grace. Produced by James Clayton and Micheal Apted. 117 minutes. Bristol Bay Productions, 2006. 1 DVD.

The Civil War. Produced by Ken Burns, 11 hours, PBS video, 1990. 5 DVD's.

UNITED STATES AND UNITED NATIONS DOCUMENTS

United Nations Development Report. The Impact of Health Insurance Coverage on Health Disparities in the United States. Human Development Report, UNDP, 2005.

U.S. Congress, "The Alien Act," July 6, 1798; Fifth Congress Enrolled Acts and Resolutions; General Records of the United States Government; Record Group 11; National Archives.

U.S. Congress, "The Victims of Trafficking and Violence Protection Act of 2000 (Public Law 106-386)," Public Law, 28 October 2000, 106th Congress. www.state.gov/documents/organization/10492.pdf, (28 October 2000).

WEBSITE SOURCES

National Underground Railroad Freedom Center, 2008, <www.freedomcenter.org/slavery-today/> (May 2008).

Merriam and Webster Dictionary and Thesaurus Online, 2008, <http://www.merriam-webster.com/> (4 April 2008).

Schweitzer, Albert. *Quotes.* 2008. <http://www.schweitzer.org/> (8 June 2008).

Vanderhaar, Gerard. *Quotes.* 2008. <http://www.gvanderhaar.org/> (13 February 2008).

Index

There are those who believe something, and therefore will tolerate nothing; and on the other hand, those who tolerate everything, because they believe nothing.

—Robert Browning

Parks, Rosa, 3
Plessy vs. Furguson, 62–63
political commentators on television, 51
political violence, 32–34
politics: practice what you preach, 63
Providence College, 46, 71

racial riots, 2, 15–17, 20, 34, 39, 46,
    64–65, 67, 101
Ray, James Earl, 12
Roger Williams University, 63
Rolland, Kayla, 26–27
Roosevelt, Franklin D.: Executive order
    9066, 62

Sacco, Ferdinando Nicola, 85
Salt Lake City mall shooting, 51
Second Amendment to the U.S.
    Constitution, 49–50, 59; stricter gun
    control laws, 59–60
Second World War, 3–4, 21n1, 62,
    71–73, 97
September 11, 2001 terrorist attacks, 2,
    53–55, 63, 70n34, 86, 98, 108
Shepard, Matthew, 27
Sirhan, Sirhan, 19, 33
Slavery, 7, 17–18, 72, 60, 91–92, 102,
    107–9, 114n6–9; present day slavery,
    107–9
Stanton, Edwin M., 91

Thompson, Eric, 29–30
Tiananmen Square Massacre, 107
torture, 9; in interrogations, 63–64

United States Constitution, x, 3, 7, 11,
    59, 63, 83, 94, 97–98
University of Texas Shooting, 1
USA Patriot Act of 2001, 98; "National
    Security Letters," 98

Vanzetti, Bartolomeo, 85
Victims of Trafficking and Violence
    Protection Act of 2000, 108
Vietnam War, 40, 55–56, 64, 90; Tet
    Offensive, 52; Vietcong, 52
violence as a sickness, 65, 68–69
violent acts, 31, 37, 49, 58, 101
Virginia Tech University Massacre, 1,
    29–31, 59, 101; victims, 31
Voting Rights Act of 1965, 8, 40

Wallace, George, 5
War on Poverty, 82
Washington, D.C. riots, 16
West Berlin, Germany, 6; fall of the
    Berlin Wall, 101
West Nickel Mines Amish School
    shooting, 27
Westside Elementary School shooting, 27
Wiesel, Elie, 73–78, 92; Feelings
    regarding God, 76–77; Seventh
    White House Millennium lecture,
    73–77; thoughts on indifference and
    violence, 73–80, 88n9–15, 88n18, 92
Wilberforce, William, 17–18, 22n35,
    60–61
Wilson, Woodrow, 97

X, Malcolm, 16

About the Author

Zachary John Martin is an Adjunct Professor of American history at Roger Williams University and Adjunct Professor of American history and American Government at Bristol Community College. He received his Bachelor's Degree in History from the University of Massachusetts Dartmouth and his Master's Degree in American history from Providence College. *The Mindless Menace of Violence* is Professor Martin's second book, and he is dedicated to the study of history and the pursuit of social change. He is the author of *Martyr to Freedom: The Life and Death of Captain Daniel Drayton* published by Hamilton Books. Professor Martin is a native of Fairhaven, Massachusetts and currently lives in Boston, Massachusetts.